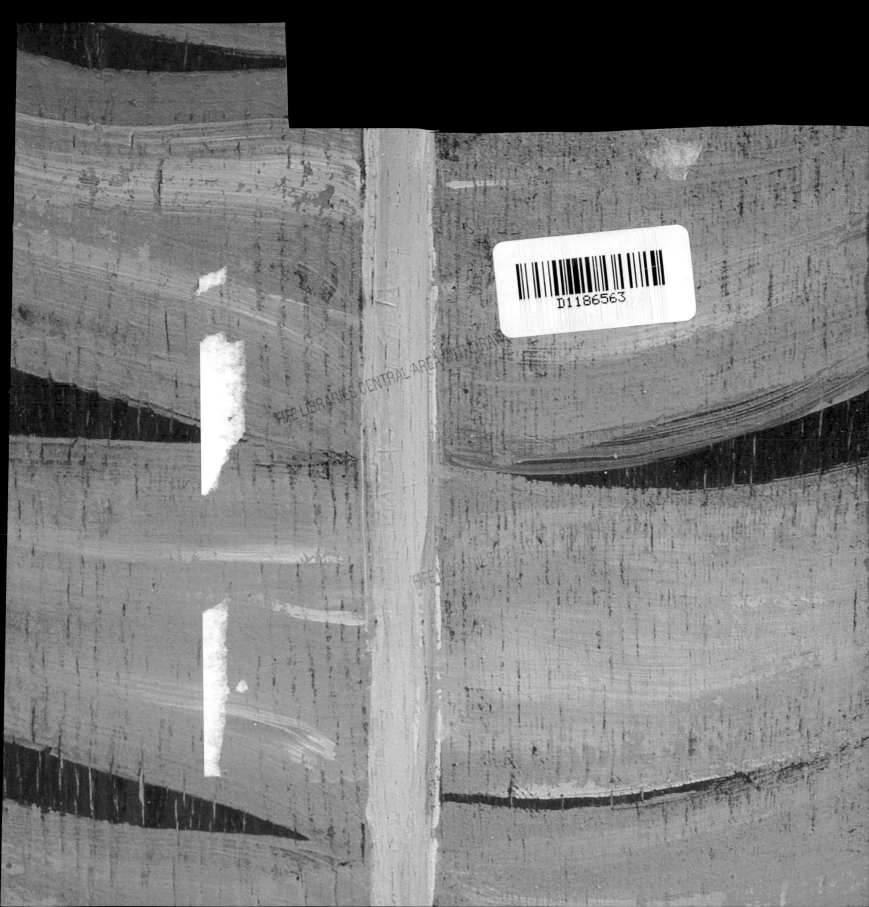

EAT CARIBBEAN

EAT CARIBBEAN VIRGINIA BURKE

SIMON & SCHUSTER

A VIACOM COMPANY

First published in Great Britain by Simon & Schuster UK Ltd, 2005
A Viacom Company
Copyright © 2005. All rights reserved.
Simon & Schuster UK Ltd, Africa House, 64–78 Kingsway, London WC2B 6AH

Text: © Walkerswood Marketing (Europe) Ltd, 2005
Design, format: © Simon & Schuster (UK) Ltd, 2005
Location photographs: © Walkerswood Marketing (Europe) Ltd, 2005
Food photographs: © Steve Baxter, 2005

1 3 5 7 9 10 8 6 4 2

Text design: Jane Humphrey
Typesetting: Stylize Digital Artwork Ltd
Photograph of Walker's Wood Village on page 125 by Ray Chen
All other location photographs by Cookie Kinkead
Food and recipe consultant: Judy Bastyra
Food photography: Steve Baxter
Home economist: Carol Tennant
Stylist for food photography: Liz Belton
Editor, indexer: Deborah Savage
Printed and bound in: Hong Kong

ISBN 0 743 25948 3 hardback
ISBN 0 743 25949 1 paperback

Contents

introduction

NYAM CARIBBEAN FOOD!

In the islands we have a cooking style that, in the past few years, has leaped into popularity and greater recognition. Suddenly there's a buzz. I have become quite caught up in this revolution by virtue of my involvement in the Caribbean food industry. This has fired up a latent passion for good food and cooking, which started in Jamaica, years ago, in my mother's kitchen.

The Caribbean has a lot to offer. There is a tremendous cultural infusion, which has influenced its food over centuries. This mélange of sometimes exotic, arresting ingredients, spices and flavours has produced some memorable dishes. Some of the regional recipes are considered 'Creole' or 'Criolla', which refers to the cooking style that evolved in the West Indies (and the southern US and Latin America) as European recipes became heavily influenced by Africans and indigenous peoples. However, many of the signature dishes have little to do with Europe and are more rooted in West Africa, India and the East.

The ingredients are probably the most fundamental element in fusing the regional cuisine together. The good news is that most of the necessary components are now available in mainstream international markets and it is easier, today, to create a real Caribbean dish wherever you are. Consult the Glossary (page 228) for description of unfamiliar items and the Caribbean names for more familiar ones.

I grew up in Jamaica, but have travelled to many other islands over the years and I've enjoyed the cooking at every level, from street food to banquets. I have no claim to expertise in the traditions of each island but it has been my privilege to share the sometimes astonishing beauty of the region with friends — a great part of this enjoyment being derived from eating the local food.

It has been a tremendous amount of fun working on the book with Judy Bastyra, Sandra Duhaney (my Walkerswood colleague) and friends who cook well. We have talked it out, shopped together, tried and tested all sorts of ingredients and recipes. Some dishes needed tweaking and some were instantly sublime. We always kept the Caribbean spirit of fun and laughter going, never taking things too seriously. Many of these sessions have evolved into parties (or 'limes' as they are known in Trinidad), as we always need people to taste and pass comment.

When entertaining at home, I choose a few complementary dishes and stay away from elaborate ones since I have a small kitchen and prefer to spend relaxed time with my guests. I will confess right now that I have had to discipline myself to measuring ingredients as I seldom used to make anything exactly the same way twice. Once you get the hang of it you will be able to adjust seasonings to your own taste. It is part of the character of Caribbean food to vary recipes from island to island. You might prefer to use more or less spice and I always adjust the robustness of my dishes according to the taste of my guests.

On the following pages are some of the most successful Caribbean dishes I have discovered, developed, teased out of my friends or resurrected from family recipes. In an effort to bring the traditional into the contemporary, I have selected these recipes by virtue of taste, ease of preparation, healthy, balanced attributes and availability of ingredients (or viable substitutes).

I thought it would be helpful to do a special section on jerk cooking (see pages 116–141) as it has become hugely popular and there are a lot of innovations derived from the authentic jerk method to explore. This is the only section where hot food reigns.

Since many excellent books on traditional Caribbean recipes are available, I don't find a need to go over that ground, but there are some classic recipes – like our beloved Ackee and Salt Fish and Rice and Peas (see pages 88 and 183) – which I feel should not be left out. Here you might notice a predominance of Jamaican recipes and this is simply because they are what I know best.

Regardless of whether you are a West Indian looking for tasty, quick, new ideas or a novice feeling inspired to dabble, I hope you will slide into the spirit of the islands and have pleasure in tasting this selection.

Virginia Burke

THE CARIBBEAN ISLANDS

Down the way where the nights are gay and the sun shines daily on the mountain top...

Harry Belafonte, 'Jamaica Farewell'

Geographically, the Caribbean cuts a wide swathe from the Florida Keys east into the Atlantic and around towards South America, linking thousands of islands. Some are tiny, projecting bravely out of the sparkling warm water, remnants of a long ago volcanic surge through the earth's crust. Islands, often so close together that they can be seen from each other's hilltops, actually cover an area of 2,500 miles. Like sisters, they seem to hold hands: from the Bahamas to the Greater Antilles, the Virgin Islands, the Leewards to the Windwards, the most easterly being Barabados, and across the south to the Lesser Antilles, together they form a loose necklace, a dotted boundary for the azure Caribbean sea.

The largest island by far is Cuba, followed by Hispaniola (made up of Haiti and the Dominican Republic), then Jamaica, Puerto Rico and Trinidad. They are best known for their sparkling blue waters and pink sandy beaches, dazzling sunsets and balmy breezes. In fact, they also boast lazy rivers, misty mountain peaks, dramatic black sand beaches, desert-like scrub, sulphur pools and deep mysterious caves.

Most islands have a calm and gentle side protected by reefs, but in direct contrast are the coastlines exposed to open sea, with restless waves and jagged coral cliffs. The 'Cayman Trough' between Jamaica and Cuba is said to be five miles deep.

Despite all these similarities there are sharp differences between the islands and even within them. It makes the Caribbean fascinating, colourful and packed with adventure. I am told that sailing through the Grenadines is the experience of a lifetime. I hope to do it.

The sea is alive with a huge variety of fish and shellfish, most of which is used in some way. Seen through recreational diving and snorkelling, or enjoyed by way of sport fishing, the daily catch is for dinner. Harvesting of the sea on a grander scale is done for commercial purposes.

The land is both cultivated and wild, with fruit, vegetables, flowers and 'bush', which are an integral part of daily life from sustenance to medicine. Large-scale agriculture is practised mostly on the bigger islands, but almost everyone with a garden has a fruit tree, maybe mangoes, coconuts or bananas, a few limes, a pepper bush and maybe a pea or two. Some smaller islands are quite flat and sandy and rely on importing most of their food.

Blessed by an agreeable balance of sun and rain, the islanders take the seasonal changes in their stride. It is warm all year round and during what are the dreariest winter months in more northerly places, we experience the best weather of all. That's when the tourists fly or sail in and bake themselves on our shores.

History of the Caribbean The record starts with the arrival of Columbus and I always take as a bit of audacity his claims of discovery when some of my ancestors were happily 'living the life' when he arrived. However, the victors write history and what took place after the arrival of Columbus created a beachhead for the West Indies, as we know it today.

Columbus was looking for a new route to India on a mission to secure a trade in precious spices, financed by Queen Isabella and King Ferdinand of Spain. He mistook the native Tainos, Arawaks, Lucayans and Caribs for 'Indians', thinking he had reached the Far East, hence the name West Indies. He arrived on San Salvador in 1492 on his first journey and raced back to Spain to prove that indeed the world was not flat and a trading route was found. It wasn't until later that they discovered the Americas lay on the way to China and India.

In 1494, Columbus arrived in Jamaica, named Xaymaca by the native Tainos, and claimed it the 'fairest island that eyes have beheld'. The islanders were shy but trusting. The relationship broke down

when mistakenly it was thought that the natives had gold. The hapless 'Indians' could produce none. They were unaccustomed to the harshness of their treatment and did not last long on any of the islands (save a settlement in Dominica), succumbing to the unceasing demands of by the invaders or the contagious diseases they brought.

The search for gold became the next mission and the trail led into South and Central America. As the treasure reaped from the region was being transported back to Spain, the Caribbean islands became trans-shipment ports and safe havens from the bloody battles fought over the bounty. Privateers and buccaneers soon roamed the turquoise sea, hijacking ships from the Spanish Main. The islands changed hands as time went on, with the arrival of the British, French and Dutch in the region.

People of the Caribbean The Spaniards settled first in Cuba and began the process of colonisation. They brought livestock and seeds. The cattle, pigs, goats and sheep thrived and their meat was immediately dried or salted for preservation in the heat. The plants that took were limes, oranges, bananas, ginger and cinnamon. Jews came with the Spaniards, fleeing the Inquisition in Europe. Many settled in the islands while others moved on to Mexico and Panama.

Once the gold started to dry up a new trade began. Slaves from the West Coast of Africa were being shackled and taken across the Atlantic, to provide cheap labour for the wealth creation of North America. In the Caribbean, the new 'gold' was sugar and tobacco and plantations for both were set up with the advent of slavery.

The British captured Jamaica from the Spanish in 1670 and eventually held the islands of the Bahamas, Cayman, some of the Virgin Islands, Antigua, Anguilla, Barbados, Bermuda, Grenada, Montserrat, St Kitts, Nevis, St Lucia, St Vincent and the Grenadines, Trinidad, Tobago, and the Turks and Caicos. They brought Irish, Scottish and Welsh managers for their plantations while the wealthy landowners usually remained in the less mosquito-infested environment of England.

Spain held Cuba, Puerto Rico and the Dominican Republic. Haiti, very early on, was the first island to gain freedom and independence – from both slavery and from France, after the famous rebellion led by Toussaint L'Ouverture; even today, Martinique, Guadeloupe and Marie Galante remain French. St Martin is also French and St Maarten is Dutch, as are Curaçao, Bonaire and Aruba. Most islands were fought over fiercely and you will find combinations of French or Spanish names and influences in British islands and so on. Most are now independent.

Early colonialists brought their favourite foods and influences, but also learned to enjoy the food that already existed, including corn, cassava and sweet potatoes. The real influence on food, though, came from the African slaves who were spread throughout the islands. With them came okras, ackees, squash and peppers. They were the cooks in the most influential kitchens and held great power over defining the appetite of the new West Indians. Their cooking became the foundation of today's Creole cuisine. Salted fish (cod, mackerel and shad) was imported as a cheap source of food for this large workforce and is considered an important staple today.

To help matters and 'mix up' the pot a little more, Indians from India and Chinese from the mainland arrived as indentured labourers. They came to work on the plantations once abolition and emancipation of slaves had been achieved. Lebanese, Syrian and Portuguese came as merchants at about the same time and I can hardly think of a nationality that has not made the islands home since then. This powerful cultural mix is the real spice of Caribbean cuisine.

The Contemporary Caribbean Lifestyle It's a funny thing, this strong feeling of solidarity that we islanders preserve, regardless of our differences in language or colour. It is particularly evident when we are away from home and everything Caribbean suddenly becomes 'ours'. We can't agree on a thing at home, where being argumentative is virtually a pastime, but take us away from 'our rocks' and the roots start clinging.

People are sometimes surprised to hear heavy accents coming from blond, blue-eyed West Indians and it is often a surprise to find combinations like Indian mixed with Lebanese and Chinese. It's also a big mistake to assume what someone will look like based on their surname. But we must be doing something right with our racial mix, because we are well known for producing world-renowned beauties.

For the most part our history was tough. There was a lot of hardship during the years of colonisation and slavery. Class and colour were brutal dividers and the gap seemed unbridgeable. But modern times don't tolerate overt discrimination and our lives are deeply intertwined. There are no secrets on a small island. One of the hardest things a newcomer has to learn, and learn quickly, is that the 'bush wire' is sharper than any modern fibre-optic communication system. News and stories travel fast. For this reason, politics is a fundamental part of daily life as we are never far removed from it.

Religion has been a strong force and the Caribbean was well covered by Christian missions from early on. But culture runs deep and in order to maintain some autonomy African slaves preserved a great many of their own spiritual customs alongside their Bible study. In Haiti, Voodoo is still tremendously powerful. Santoria in Cuba mixes Catholic saints with black magic. Obeah in Jamaica runs right through the island, though mostly out of sight. Churches exist side by side with synagogues, mosques and temples and with a little observation you will find an equal number of rum bars for those who get their spirit elsewhere.

A lot has changed in a short time. Up to a few years ago many of the wealthier West Indians

continued to send their children to Europe for higher education. This is less so now that we have the University of the West Indies and more students venture north to the US and Canada. Since the advent of cable TV in particular, and easy air travel, the influence from North America has grown much greater.

Our children on the whole get a decent education. West Indians have excelled in just about every field and many large countries have

benefited from our distinguished scientists, doctors, athletes, artists, musicians, writers and even military experts. People are much better off now than before and there is a greater social mobility, which enables people to rise out of the ashes of disinheritance and be self-determining.

Caribbean people have always had a strong style of their own. Be it in food, music, clothing, house colour or hairstyles, we have set a hot pace. If we have one thing in common, it is that we love to party and take every opportunity to celebrate. We enjoy dance, theatre, parades, carnivals and street fetes.

Carnival in Trinidad brings thousands of people flocking every year for a one-week bacchanal. The bright costumes and self-expression go way back and each island has its calendar of such events. Few of these pass without generous feasts of some sort, be it street food on the parade route or a proper 'feed' after. I've yet to hear of a Caribbean person with a family who died or got married without some form of celebration involving food. Happily, a lot of the annual and rite-of-passage traditions have been passed down, offering opportunities for young and old, rich and poor to mix (and multiply!). We don't need much of an excuse to gather, eat, drink and be merry.

All celebrations are also defined by music, whether it be a military band, the traditional 'mento' or calypso combo, steel band, reggae or dance-hall sound system. We sing, dance and clap hands joyfully, even in church.

We like sports and games and we get pretty crazy about dominoes, horse betting and even mah-jongg (mainly the Chinese). Jamaicans get soccer silly during the World Cup and Cubans excel in baseball. The islands always have great representation in international track and field events and let me not forget to mention those critical days, for men and women alike, during the annual Test Cricket matches, when things virtually come to a standstill. Casual Sunday cricket matches are perfect for picnics.

Since the climate is usually very cooperative, a lot of entertaining is done outdoors. Somehow, a pot of 'mannish water' (goat-head soup) being prepared for a ground-breaking would not be the same cooked inside the kitchen. The roast suckling pig won't fit in the oven. Our events are generally speaking very casual, but we also love the pomp of ceremony and do know how to button up and get formal.

Today, most people live closely as small families and quite often at least one grandparent is part of the unit. Breakfast was traditionally quite a heavy or substantial meal but now, with so many women working outside the home, this has changed. Where it used to be porridge and cooked food, we grab a bowl of cornflakes and a cup of instant coffee and head out the door. Nowadays, lunch is regularly purchased from a fast food restaurant or street vendor. By evening though, there is usually a 'dutchie' (large iron pot) on the stove, since as families we seldom eat out at dinnertime.

On Saturdays, it is quite traditional to make a big soup (this might come from the Jewish tradition) with vegetables left over at the week's end added. Sunday is a quiet day, with the main meal of the week the centre of family activity. It is served a bit late, after church or after a morning at the beach. We visit each other without much formality and whatever food is available is stretched generously to accommodate anyone who passes by.

Today, not as much time is spent in the kitchen as before and I know quite a few young women who have skipped the ritual of learning how to cook and entertain as their mothers did. But, to balance this somewhat, more men are taking an interest in cooking (mainly the meat course) so it is not seen solely as a woman's domain. This faster, new lifestyle has certainly impacted on our cuisine and we may get the traditional specialities only occasionally. It has made us no less demanding when it comes to the quality of our food, but the time spent in preparation has changed.

A Childhood Memory I have only happy recollections of the summer holidays spent on my grandparents' farm, along with my cousins, in Falmouth, Jamaica. It was primarily a dairy, with some pimento trees, but they grew everything else they needed. The smell of the tack room, where they kept corn for the chickens in sacks, mixed with the leather saddles stored in the cool, stone basement is one of those unique olfactory memories I still can't shake.

All our meals were cooked over a wood-burning stove in a kitchen separated from the house, as was common in the old days. It was hot 'chocolate tea' and porridge for breakfast each morning and with such a pack of boisterous grandchildren to feed, I don't know how my grandmother coped. We roamed the property all day and got into every imaginable scrape that children could. We rode on the donkey cart, drank coconut water and ate jellies and raided way too many guinep and hog plum trees. We ate 'until wi belly buss'.

When our parents came to collect us after a week or two, we had the grand family reunion around a very large table groaning with dishes of tasty food such as pumpkin soup with rolls, roast beef with gravy, roasted chicken or duck, rice and peas, roasted breadfruit and plantain. There was cho-cho, green beans, avocado, salad, and maybe a fruit salad or bread pudding with lots of raisins.

My grandfather held court. He sat at the head of the table with a side-plate featuring one freshly picked scotch bonnet pepper waiting to accompany every bite. Not a word was spoken or a morsel touched until he said grace and had taken the first helping.

In later years when they moved to Kingston, my grandpa cultivated vegetables in the back end of his urban garden. He patiently tended corn, peas, callaloo, peppers (of course), lettuce, tomatoes, carrots, onions, escallion (our name for spring onions) and whatever else he fancied. None of his remaining children (of 13) would want for some fresh bundle when they visited. I loved spending hours with him under the tamarind tree after school. He died there one afternoon, in his hammock.

One thing for sure I got from my grandfather is the love of a fresh scotch bonnet pepper on the plate.

MARKETS OF THE CARIBBEAN

A famous saying in Trinidad: 'the island where birds speak French, oysters grow on trees and the flowers bloom at night'.

Once you have arrived in a Caribbean town or village the most colourful and lively spot to check out will be the market. Usually open from very early in the morning, this is the hub where all the fresh produce will arrive from the nearby countryside, and goods, cash and news will be exchanged for a few hours. The supermarkets cannot compete with either the freshness, variety, price of goods or critical point of communication. From memory, it is the least altered part of our towns.

In a typical Jamaican or Haitian market the abundance of ripe fruit and vegetables will be arranged in attractive displays on crocus bags (hessian) or in large straw baskets padded with banana 'trash' (dried banana leaves). Many of the market women (as it is usually women on these islands) have retained their colourful head ties, multicoloured skirts and blouses and the ever-present apron with deep pockets full of change. There's a knife for cutting portions of yam, sugar cane or fingers of bananas, a tin cup (quite often still measuring in gills) for scooping peas and a scale (probably shared) to make sure you can see that she has given you a few ounces extra, known as 'brawta'.

If you go into a really large bustling market, such as Coronation Market in downtown Kingston, the first thing that will hit you is the smell – a pungent mix of freshly harvested food and spices mixed with the aroma of cooking and humanity. Next to assail your senses is the dizzying colour – the bright orange of cut pumpkins becomes almost psychedelic beside the green of young bananas, multicoloured mangoes, the earthy browns of yams and purples of sweet potatoes. Red, green and yellow peppers are displayed in small hills.

And if your head is not spinning yet, you will note the cacophony. Everyone seems to be shouting and especially if you are new on the scene it will seem like everyone needs your immediate attention. The music system will be rocking at full pitch from one or more corners. There is a strong sensation of being in Africa, in these markets.

Apart from food, you will be able to buy just about everything you need for your house. Hand-made tin graters for coconut, coal-pots, dutch pots, multicoloured plastic buckets and bowls, straw brooms, woven floor mats, dusters, oil lamps, cooking spoons and scrubbing brushes. Fresh fish, live chickens, fresh eggs. If you are in Haiti, you will probably be thoroughly distracted by the fascinating paintings, tinwork and craft.

It is not uncommon for goods to arrive at these markets packed in hampers and loaded on a donkey, especially in rural areas, but far more often now, the country bus is the preferred means of transport. It virtually defies science how the loads on top of the buses or 'tap taps' (in Haiti) stay in place through the journeys down steep and winding country roads.

When you are in Curaçao, one of the big attractions is the floating market where goods arrive on boats. As Curaçao is very arid, the boats come in from Venezuela regularly with fresh produce and fish. They tie up alongside the dock in Willemstad and all the vegetables you could want are attractively displayed under tarpaulins, the length of the street. The vendors are Spanish-speaking young men. The fish and conch are sold directly off the decks of the boats where there is refrigeration. It is very quaint and, as with most markets, at its best first thing in the morning. Willemstad is quite astonishing and picturesque as you approach from the airport, with buildings that are colourful and distinctively Dutch in design.

On a recent visit to the Plaza de Mercado in Puerto Rico I found a very organised market in an old and attractive open-sided iron building. Across the street on the market square are a few butcher shops for convenience. Though the produce was basically the same as on other islands, I noticed many unusual varieties of plantains, yams and peppers. The cinnamon sticks were at least 18 inches long and they had the largest pineapples I have ever seen. Ripe fruits and vegetable sectors, with a fresh juice and snack counter, define the market, and dried and herbal seasonings and remedies are separate. You'll also find a great variety of spices like annatto (roucou), rosemary, oregano, purple basil, bay, nutmeg, cloves, anise and mustard seed. There are dried beans, peanuts, sesame and pumpkin seeds, malangueta (herbs of paradise), and some hardware, like the plantain press which I purchased from a charming Mexican. No Puerto Rican (or Cuban) market would be complete without guava paste – a sweet sticky confection.

One corner held natural remedies like aloe, vetiver, various roots, bushes and religious candles and I get the feeling that the stallholder acts as an unofficial dispensary with his knowledge of cures.

If it is the vast catalogue of herbs, spices and staples that unite Caribbean kitchens, it is the different use of these flavours which define the high notes of each island's specialities. Greater employment of hot peppers or strong spices is evident in the more African-influenced islands. This might be a bit of a generalisation, but I find Spanish, particularly Cuban and Puerto Rican cooking a lot milder and more subtle. The French style is a bit more mysterious and I really give the Haitians credit for making even the simplest dish, such as 'djon-djon' (mushroom and rice, taste so sophisticated. (Both modern Haitian and Cuban cooks have learned to cook with far less imported food than on most of the other islands.)

As I said, though, this use of hot pepper is probably just a personal observation as it is quite an individual thing and pepper sauce is usually available on the side. You should remember too that a scotch bonnet pepper (also called 'country pepper') can give a huge amount of taste to a dish without releasing any heat, if it is left undisturbed to cook with the food and not allowed to break. In Trinidad they cut up 'seasoning peppers' and use them for flavour as they have no heat.

Curry comes to us through our Indian population. The curries vary in intensity and colour and are particularly widespread in Trinidad, where curry is used in a variety of foods. In Jamaica, though curry is very popular, you won't see much being curried besides goat (a speciality) or chicken, unless it is on an Indian menu.

In Guadeloupe, their version of curry dishes are called 'colombo', made with a unique blend of milder curry spices that is used to flavour all kinds of meat including goat, and also vegetables like aubergine. There is a charming spice market in downtown Pointe-à-Pitre, where colombo and many other flavourings can be found.

Seasoning is basically down to spring onions, garlic, onions, chives, shallots, hot peppers, thyme, oregano, chandon beni, coriander, salt, sweet and hot peppers. Many, many savoury dishes use them. Various combinations of these spices give us the unique flavours used locally like 'adobo', 'sauce chien', 'ti-malice' or 'jerk'. It is in the marinating with these seasonings where most meat dishes get their depth of flavour.

Part of the inheritance from harder times sees the use of small portions of smoked meat or fish to impart flavour. Many bean dishes, soups and even vegetable stews use the intensity of pig's tail, salt beef or fish.

Other popular flavours used for both sweet and savoury dishes come from ginger, coconut, nutmeg, mace, vanilla, tamarind, limes, allspice and rum. We are not purists, however, and Caribbean markets and groceries are well supplied with all-purpose seasonings containing monosodium glutamate. For a quick stock we often rely on noodle soup packets and seasoning cubes.

We like to colour our food and use several natural sources like annatto, turmeric, saffron, paprika, caramel and soy sauce or commercial products like 'browning' popularly used for meat dishes. For confectionery, bright artificial colourings like greens, blues or pinks can be found to dye coconut sweets or icing.

As you can see, many of the ingredients you will need to make a delicious Caribbean meal are quite common, everyday items. However, there are many exotic fruits and vegetables and some indigenous fish and wildlife that are not available beyond our shores and this is mainly because they do not travel well and are best experienced in their local environment. So, I hope this gives you yet another reason to come to our beautiful islands and have a taste of our unique hospitality.

I took a trip on a sailing ship and when I reached Jamaica I made a stop... Harry Belafonte, 'Jamaica Farewell'

POPULAR STREET FOOD AND BEACH FOOD

One of the ways travellers discover a new culture is to get on the ground, walk the streets and talk to the people. One very good way of mingling is through street food. See it, smell it, touch it and taste it.

On the islands, our lifestyle is very conducive to outdoor mixing, cooking and sidewalk shopping. We spend a lot of time just hanging out on the street. In the smaller communities we might spend the evening keeping cool by sitting on a wall or bench, catching up and sharing news with our friends (otherwise known as gossip or 'suss'). Along the sea wall in Havana (along the Malecon), Cuban people hang out until the wee hours every night. We often stop at the gate as we walk past and chat to our neighbours. The dogs bob and weave amongst the children who will claim a quiet street for their ball games. A boy on a bicycle articulates his skill, for all the girls to admire.

Particularly in Cuba and Jamaica the music boxes are aimed outward and entertain (or irritate) all within earshot. In rural areas it is not uncommon to see goats or chickens wondering about in the mix — it is all part of Caribbean street life. It is something that we miss terribly when we travel to big cities, especially if we have grown up this way.

Most street food vendors fall into two categories: some are mobile and move from place to place with their goods. They operate using carts or bikes or walk around peddling fresh fruit, ice creams, chips, nuts or other snacks. The other kind are self-styled 'cooks' who set-up in any location where they feel they can attract a clientele. Sometimes the food is cooked at home, at other times prepared on the spot. If the offer is good and word carries, they might continue to operate, casually, in the same spot for many years. The clientele will go out of their way to patronise a favourite vendor. It is often a very rustic experience, so the best advice I can give is that you eat from a set-up that looks well established and observes good hygiene. If there is a strong following of eager customers the food is

more likely to be fresh and will probably be a delicious experience. I am happy to report that, like my friends, I eat quite freely from established vendors and have never had reason to regret it. Use your discretion.

One of the fascinating aspects of outdoor food vendors, besides some of the unique foods offered, are the inventive devices and cooking methods that can be found. Coal-pots (a small, one-pot stove used outdoors), woks, griddles, jerk pans and mobile roasters – to name a few.

Think of the way that your Mum's home-made versions couldn't compete with fast food burgers or pizza; most popular street food loses its attraction in the same way when you try to replicate it at home (sorry, Mum!). It has a lot to do with the atmosphere and that elusive, serendipitous ingredient that cannot be packaged. For this reason, I will only try to describe for you some of the more memorable experiences and leave the recipes safely with the vendors. There are many specialities and each island has its strong traditions; Jamaica, Trinidad, Tobago and Puerto Rico have well-developed street-food cultures.

On most islands, you will find that the 'coconut water man' is a popular stop in the heat of the day. They used to move around with pushcarts piled high with coconuts and a 'palm' frond standing tall like a flag. Nowadays they set up stalls on the roadside. The vendor will pull a cold 'jelly coconut' from an 'ice box' – a large metal-lined container or old cooler in which a large block of ice and water can chill the young green coconuts. If experienced, the vendor will deftly slash the thick outer layer at the top of the coconut with about three strokes of his sharp machete and the final whack will expose a small hole in the shell without spilling a drop of the nutritious and refreshing liquid inside. It is nothing like coconut milk. It is not exactly sweet and surprisingly it does not really have a strong coconut flavour – it is hard to describe, but you'll be startled at how filling and satisfying a cold 'jelly' can be.

To consume the traditional way, spread your legs apart and bend forward, cover the hole with your lips and then, in one motion, tip your head and the coconut back and start guzzling. You will have to do this a few times if there is a lot of 'water' and be prepared to have the clear juice running down your face and neck until you become an expert. (If you don't enjoy that kind of rustic challenge, chances are a plastic straw can be produced.) When you have drained the coconut, give it back to the man and watch as he chops it in two, skilfully, stopping just short of his hand. He'll then give it back to you with a chip of coconut husk to use as a scoop. Use that and rake out the soft jelly inside. This is the prize. After a little initiation you'll be able to enjoy the experience like a pro.

Your coconut jelly may be at any of the stages of development – from barely there, clear and slippery or white and chewy, looking more like the mature coconut that most people are accustomed to. When you buy a coconut in a shop, it will most likely be fully developed.

Coconut water is now sold bottled but this is not a patch on drinking it straight from Mother Nature's cup. Rum and coconut water used to be quite trendy, but people drink coconut water now more as a healthy option and a fresh young coconut is considered quite beneficial if you are ill. You will find coconuts everywhere throughout Caribbean.

In Jamaican towns such as Kingston or Montego Bay, mobile street vendors like the peanut man push their carts to a popular location. That could simply be a spot where traffic stalls for the lights. He operates fast as his customers might not actually stop moving while making the purchase. You are aware of his presence because his roaster lets out steam that activates a shrill whistle on the cart. The freshly roasted peanuts are warm, delicious, and deftly packed in a brown paper cone.

Ice cream, icicle (frozen popsicle) and 'sno-cone' (shaved ice with syrup, also known as 'sky juice' or 'suck-suck') carts are moved around the town in an effort to keep us cool. Other popular street side stalls sell a variety of fruit, biscuits, buns and cheese and bags of banana chips.

Some Jamaican vendors have 'cook shacks' like at Faith's Pen en route to Ocho Rios travelling from Kingston, where there is a line-up of stalls and a range of food. From early in the morning you will find roasted or boiled corn, roasted breadfruit, yam, ackee and salt fish, callaloo, 'pan chicken' (barbecue), fried fish, 'bammies', 'festivals' and soup. The tradesmen and travellers who don't want a long stop heavily patronise this lay-by. It's time to *nyam* some food!

One of the best 'pan-chicken' stops you'll find is on Red Hills Road in Kingston, on a Friday night. The sidewalk is lined with makeshift barbecues made from oil drums, teaming with people, swirling in smoke and the aroma of succulent chicken. This is served up in a foil package so be prepared to lick your fingers.

You can cross the island of Jamaica eating like Pac-man if you know where to stop. From Mandeville to Kingston on the street side lay-by you will find salt fish and steaming-hot, roasted yam that is topped with a little margarine. It is particularly good when the day is still a little chilly and misty, as it can be in the cooler climes of Manchester in the early morning or even late afternoon. Look out for steaming pots of specials like banana porridge near YS Falls.

At Middle Quarters, in St Elizabeth, many vendors will rush to your car with plastic bowls of seriously hot peppered shrimp. If you are a true lover of peppery food these shrimp will disappear long before you reach Savannah La Mar or Negril. Pick up a cold, sweet drink to put out the fire.

Many people will drive for hours to Boston Bay in Portland (the opposite side of the island) for jerk pork, sausage and chicken – it is said to be the home of jerk and many people believe that the authentic recipe has never left.

Hellshire Beach and Port Royal are best known for 'fried fish and bammy' (cassava cakes) but you will also find lobster, crab, conch and even small oysters. At night in the old port, the vendors sit on stools around the square with their tilly lamps and glass boxes filled with fried sprats and bammy, awaiting the people who drive out along the causeway in the evening just to take in some salt air and buy a fish. You will get yours on a piece of paper. The fish are whole and crisply fried. You are supposed to eat everything, as even the bones are crunchy. That is the pass-by visit; otherwise there are rustic sidewalk, rooftop and dockside eateries nearby specialising in seafood, where you can sit down for a very informal meal.

Many beaches have knocked-together stands, often made of bamboo or weathered wood and covered with zinc or thatched with palm. I am totally at home here. There are no doors and the floor is sand. I am barefoot. Since the stall is usually no more than 50 feet from where the fishing boats pull in you are assured of getting the freshest catch around. The fish is simply seasoned and deep-fried in a large wok or roasted over an open wood or coal fire. Most of the time, you get to pick your fish, but don't be in a hurry as this is not 'fast' food. I promise you it is well worth the wait.

In Trinidad, street-food stalls flourish. Some of the most popular dishes are East-Indian-style foods like rotis (stuffed with a variety of curried fillings such as lamb, chicken, beef or potatoes). 'Doubles' are two small 'pancakes' with a curried chick-pea filling and chutney and – if you are lucky – a shredded coconut topping. 'Phulouri' is a fried dumpling with similar texture to a doughnut and you'll get a bagful with mango sauce for a snack. These are all easily found.

You'll see stalls on the roadside with dried or preserved fruit and sweets and large jars of pickled plums, green mango and pineapple. I love the 'pommes ce theure', which are green June plums in brine with chandon beni (a herb almost identical in flavour to coriander). They are crisp, delicious and simply moreish, but I think you might have to plan a trip to Trinidad for that snack!

In the evenings, all around the Savannah, a large recreational field in Port of Spain, a popular street event takes place. Stalls are set up and vendors sell all kinds of consumables from coconuts to oysters. On the street in St James where the music and 'lime' (party) spills on to the sidewalk, watch out for corn soup, rotis and, nowadays, jerk chicken.

ICE COLD
Stag
Carib
Malta
Shandy
Royal
Guinness
Heineken
Mackeson
Carlsberg
Ginseng Up
Soft Drinks
Fresh Orange Juice

VILMA'S
HOT BAKE ᴺ SHARK

The most popular beach, Maracas, is home to the most famous Trinidadian beach food called 'shark and bake'. I find it funny that, though people call it that, all the signs announce 'bake and shark' and no one, so far, has explained why. (Jamaicans say 'rice and peas' and the 'Trinis' say 'peas and rice'; it's the same silliness.) A 'bake' is a kind of fried flat bread, though there are baked bakes and coconut bakes too. Delicious, but quite different in texture. You will be offered a wide variety of sauces and fillings, to top your sandwich off. When I went recently, Vilma had the best on offer at the beach and she cooks to order. You will get fresh salad items like cucumber, tomatoes and lettuce, mango chutney, tamarind or garlic sauce, 'kutchula' (a kind of mango pickle), chandon beni, pepper sauce, honey mustard, garlic and creamy dressing to garnish with. The sandwiches are so good some people find it hard to eat just one. I have bent my own rule here and given a recipe for coconut bakes (see page 177).

On Tobago, which still remains very unspoilt, Store Bay has all the offerings of Trinidad's street food and some, but also features flying fish as a speciality.

Street Food in Puerto Rico is somewhat more concentrated than on the other islands. A very popular area is in Pinones, just east of San Juan on route 187. Stall after stall along the beach road offers a variety of fried foods, seafood, roast pork, coconuts and other cold drinks. This area purportedly offers the most African-influenced of Puerto Rican food. At last count there were about 75 such shacks and bars with varying degrees of rustic appeal. This is a very popular venue, particularly on weekends, and the first thing to try is probably a 'bacalaito'. This is a salt-cod fritter, very crisply fried and nearly the size of a Frisbee. Or try an 'alcapurria', which is cassava dough stuffed with meat or crab. The food is tasty but very greasy, so I'm told that you should only indulge yourself occasionally if you want to stay on the beach volleyball team.

The snacks are not particularly hot or spicy but you will find bottles of pickled peppers on the tables everywhere, so peppery heat is quite optional. Another speciality of the beach is 'pionono', a ring of fried plantain stuffed with a tomato and crab mixture ('salmorejo'), topped with batter and then deep-fried. It is very filling.

Back in Old San Juan, the street food is much lighter. If you happen on a street festival you will find pina coladas, lots of sweets, ice creams, plantain chips and cotton candy.

You can drive about 45 minutes from San Juan into the mountains to Guavate to eat 'lechonera', or pig on a spit. It is a very popular place for Sunday family outings because there is a choice of food for everyone. They even have 'pavochon', which is turkey done the same way. The pork is seasoned with adobo spices and roasted until the crackling is crisp and the meat moist and delicious.

Other Puerto Rican specialities are 'pastilles', mashed plantain stuffed with ground beef or chicken, wrapped in banana leaf and paper, tied with string and steamed. (We have something similar in Jamaica but it is sweet, called 'blue drawers', or 'duckanoo'.) You will find salt-fish salad, yellow rice and beans, stewed tripe and 'cassava escabeche' (escoveitched, that is, pickled, cassava), which I found particularly delicious. Picnic benches are the order of the day and you can move from restaurant to restaurant as they are all open-sided and easily accessible to the activity on the street.

One of the most irresistible treats is the local 'helados' (ice-cream) in Ponce on the south coast. There you'll find an unhurried line of patrons waiting their turn outside a small shop (opposite the old red and black fire-station) on the main square. It was hard to choose from coconut, guanabana, tamarind and

peanut (and there were many other choices). We licked our cones as we walked around and then, succumbing to temptation, we went back for more. I don't think I have ever had more delicious ice cream.

COOK'S NOTES

Cook's tips also appear throughout, within individual recipes.

Measuring It won't really make a difference if you use a large onion, potato or tomato instead of a medium one, or if you use two tablespoons of parsley instead of one. Quantities of some ingredients are more a matter of taste or convenience, so use your common sense.

However, I'd recommend that you stick to exact measurements with baked recipes and desserts as those results are based on precision.

Pots, pans and knives I thank my mother for drumming into my head the value of owning a few good pots. They will last forever if you invest in good quality. Best bets are heavy-bottomed stainless-steel saucepans, a good cast-iron skillet and a solid dutch-pot or 'dutchie' (a heavy iron pot with a cover). You will also need an oven-roasting pan occasionally. If you love stir-fry, get a wok. These pots will do most of the work. A cook's best friend will be a good set of knives. I love my cleaver, but it's not essential if you have a good medium knife for slicing and chopping and a small one for paring and peeling. Just keep them sharp.

Grills I have fallen in love with my stovetop grill pan. I enjoy cooking quickly and nothing quite gives you the control of browning (without too much oil) and getting that sear without lighting a barbecue. Sometimes you need to go under flame (grill) so you'll need a rack over the roasting pan; otherwise, coal or gas barbecue grills will do the trick outdoors.

Cooking oil I have become accustomed to using olive oil for much of my cooking, but it is really only necessary in dressings or pasta where the flavour shines. Coconut oil, which lends fabulous flavour to fried foods, rundowns and oiled downs, used to be more popular. Use lighter oil like corn, soy or groundnut, especially for frying.

Nothing finishes eggs, a sauce or mashed staples like butter. I have virtually abandoned margarine. If you are cooking with butter and don't want it to burn, mix in a little oil.

Vinegar We usually use white vinegar, such as cane vinegar, for pickles and salads, but some dishes benefit from less acidic vinegars like red or white wine or even balsamic, all of which have made their way into our modern kitchens.

Seasonings and spices I try for fresh herbs wherever possible, be it thyme or oregano. However, sometimes we only have dry herbs on hand. Use a bit less, as they tend to be more potent. Abandon the garnish if you can't get fresh parsley, basil or cilantro since dry leaves won't work at the finish line (use finely chopped spring onion tops in a pinch). Whenever you see 'chopped spring onions' in recipes it means use both green and white parts. Try to use fresh-ground black pepper when possible, unless I have specified white pepper. For hot peppers, I have kept it to a medium level, to keep the dish friendly. Heat is always optional: even with a spicy dish like jerk you can adjust the level. Don't get too caught up on the scotch bonnet issue, use hot chillies or hot pepper sauce as a substitute but choose a sauce that's not too vinegary or it will bring a sour note to the taste.

Citrus fruit It goes for limes, lemons and sour oranges, too, that you can interchange them unless it is the main ingredient of the dish.

Washing chicken When I say, 'wash the chicken', everyone knows what I mean at home. When I say it overseas, people often look at me as if a significant part had dropped off my face. As Caribbean people, what we do with chicken, regardless of whether it is freshly butchered, presented in a Styrofoam tray or wrapped up in waxy paper from the best delicatessen in town, is to wash it. Wash with salted water, with vinegar or in a bath of lime juice (no rinsing necessary). For whatever reasons, it is standard procedure and we insist on it. Pat dry and then get on with the seasoning. Trust me, it will taste better.

Seasoning meat and poultry This single process is at the heart of Caribbean flavour. Rub the spices in and leave to marinate. Think of planting in late summer and waiting through winter for a glorious harvest in the spring.

Preparing dried salt fish or smoked red herring Dried, salted fish (usually cod) is a popular ingredient. It is quite easy to prepare for use. When you find dried salt fish it often looks like whitish cardboard. Most often it is left to soak in cold water overnight. I usually just rince it off under the cold tap then place it in a pan full of water and bring to the boil. Throw that water away, fill up the pot again and boil once more. Drain and cool, remove skin (if any) then using two forks or your fingers, flake into little pieces. You might have to remove bones, or you can buy it boneless.

Don't try to take out all the salt or you'll miss the point of your dish. Buy ready-prepared salt fish canned (also known as 'bacalao' or 'morue') if you'd prefer.

You can buy smoked herring as small, oily, salty, fillets. So you'll only need to pour boiling water over the fillets in a bowl and let them sit for 10 minutes in the water, before draining. Do this twice if you think it is still too salty. Proceed to flake and de-bone as with salt fish, before using.

Making coconut milk If you choose to buy a fresh coconut, and this is a good choice, pick one that is heavy (fully mature) and shake and listen to make sure it is full of liquid. They can last like this for months.

To break the coconut, you'll need a little force. (I often stand on the top step and bowl it on to the concrete in the garden, but then I have to go searching for the pieces.) Use a sharp ice pick to punch holes in two of the 'eyes' and allow the water to drain away. Then strike it between the eyes to break the shell. Then use a paring knife to prise the white meat away from the shell.

This needs to be grated (use a blender). I recommend you do a few pieces, at a time, adding water. Strain off, pressing the grated flesh into a sieve or piece of muslin while collecting the milky liquid. The strength of your coconut milk depends on the amount of water used. You can make it very creamy, which is good for desserts. A good guideline is to use twice the volume of water as you have of grated coconut. The measurements I have given in recipes are suitable for using standard canned coconut milk.

To make dessicated coconut for baking, you'll need to peel off the brown skin and only grate the white part.

Now you've got the tools, come with me and let's *nyam* Caribbean!

appetisers

TEASERS, TANTALISERS & NIBBLES

West Indians love to entertain visitors. We like sharing our culture and will immediately want to introduce our guests to our specialities. The chances are, you'll be given a cool drink in the shade immediately on arrival and you won't be in the Caribbean long before someone offers you a titbit.

The arrival of a relative or guest from abroad is a good enough excuse to take time off from work and gather a group of friends on the patio. More often than not this will develop into a drinking session and, though you might have started with freshly squeezed limeade, offers of beer or rum will soon be made. Bar drinks call for salty snacks and these can vary in size and complexity, depending on the type of occasion and how long it is before the next meal. These snacks are called 'cutters' in Trinidad. You will get all kinds of crispy and crunchy nibbles: roasted peanuts or cashews; fried banana or plantain or coconut chips; or fishy dishes like Trinadian Bul Jol – similar to Jamaican 'Pick up Salt Fish' – (see page 47) or Solomon Gundy (see page 45) served on crackers; ackra (salt fish) fritters or salsa dips.

If it is a cocktail party at sunset, we'll up the ante and bring on the finger food like ackee canapés, escoveitch fish, cocktail patties, meatballs, prawns, smoked marlin, stuffed eggs and crab cakes. Stay around a bit and some of these party dishes, when presented at dinnertime, might become starters.

Avocado Dip (Guacamole)

Avocados are known as 'pears' on the English-speaking islands and are usually eaten very simply, sliced and served with salt and pepper (often eaten with every meal during the season) or mashed between two slices of bread. This practice came about because avocado was used as a substitute for butter in the old days before refrigeration. The West Indian varieties tend to be quite large, with a very creamy flesh.
Preparation time: 10 minutes. Serves 4–6

2 small avocados or one large Caribbean avocado, halved and stoned

1 large tomato, de-seeded and chopped

1 onion, finely diced

1 tbsp freshly squeezed lime juice (lemon can be substituted)

2 tbsp finely chopped fresh coriander

1/2–1 tsp hot pepper sauce

salt and pepper

1. Scoop the flesh of the avocado(s) into a bowl. Add all the other ingredients and mix together (allow the avocado flesh to remain a little chunky). Keep chilled until ready to serve.
2. Serve with plantain chips or Tostones (see page 172).

Black Bean Dip

Cuba

Black beans are a fundamental part of the diet in the Spanish-speaking islands. This dip is Cuban influenced.
Preparation time: 15 minutes. Serves: 6–10/makes about 500 ml/2 cups

425 g/15 oz cooked black beans

1 garlic clove, chopped finely

60 ml/1/4 cup soured cream or natural yogurt

3 tbsp chopped fresh coriander, plus 1 tbsp to garnish

a dash of hot pepper sauce (optional)

a pinch of salt

1. Drain the beans thoroughly and blend to a paste in a food processor with the other ingredients.
2. Garnish with the coriander and serve with corn chips, mini toasts or crudités.

Curried Salt Fish Dip

This dip is similar to Gundy Cream Cheese Dip (see Cook's note, page 45) but much more tangy! It is always very well received.

Preparation time: 25 minutes cooking or overnight soaking for salt fish + 20 minutes softening cheese + 15 minutes.
Serves 4–6

225 g/8 oz Philadelphia cream cheese

175 g/6 oz prepared salt fish or canned bacalao, drained

1 firm tomato, de-seeded and chopped finely

1 onion, finely chopped or grated

1 garlic clove, pressed

2 tbsp curry paste

juice and grated zest of 1 lime or lemon

1 tsp hot pepper sauce or very finely chopped hot pepper

2 tbsp finely chopped fresh coriander or parsley, to garnish

1.   Leave the cheese to soften, unrefrigerated, for 15–20 minutes as this will make it easier to mix.
2.   Meanwhile, prepare the salt fish as directed (see page 39) or drain canned bacalao .
3.   Add to the cream cheese using a fork. Mix in all rest of ingredients also using a fork, checking for taste. You may prefer more or less lime juice, hot pepper or curry. Make sure it is well combined. (If you use a processor it will become a bit runny – it will taste the same, but it is nicer when firm.)
4.   Place in a bowl and chill until ready to serve.
5.   Sprinkle with the coriander or parsley to garnish. Try serving this with crudités.

Solomon Gundy

Known fondly as 'Gundy', this is a spread made from salted smoked herring/or shad) and spices. This speciality goes way back in our heritage. Some say the word comes from salmagundis, a finely chopped salad of mixed ingredients that originated at the court of Louis XIV in France.

Nowadays Gundy can be found bottled and ready to be eaten on crackers as a salty snack with drinks. Quite spicy, it is used in much the same way as Gentleman's Relish (anchovy butter spread). It is difficult to break the cycle once you have started nibbling and quenching your thirst, which makes it a favourite at bars. For many, as with anchovies, Gundy is an acquired taste.

See page 96 for succulent Gundy Pasta.

Preparation time: 1–2 hours soaking + 10 minutes

125 g/4 oz (about 4–5) dried smoked herring fillets
½ onion
½–1 scotch bonnet pepper, de-seeded
4 tsp cane vinegar or distilled (white) malt vinegar
3 tsp vegetable oil

1. Soak the herring in cold water for an hour and then taste. Change the water and soak some more only if it is still too salty. The herring should still be quite salty when you stop the soaking process. See page 39 for hot-water method.
2. Flake the flesh with your fingers or two forks.
3. Either finely chop the ingredients and mix together (my preference) or blend everything in a food processor (makes it very smooth).

Cook's tips: Gundy can be eaten with crackers or toast and will keep well for at least a month, refrigerated in a tightly sealed jar.

To make Gundy Cream Cheese Dip, mix 225 g/8 oz softened Philadelphia cream cheese with 2–3 tbsp Solomon Gundy with a fork and use a rubber spatula to scrape together. Chill in a pretty bowl or a red cabbage leaf and then serve with crackers or crudités. This gentle introduction to Gundy inevitably escalates into a mad craving.

Pick-up Saltfish (Jamaica) or Bul Jol (Trinidad)

Jamaica + Trinidad

This finely chopped salad can be made with either salt fish or smoked herring and is popular from Jamaica to Trinidad. The name changes, and occasionally a few of the ingredients (for example boiled eggs or avocado are sometimes used) but whenever you get kissed by the lime and the pepper this startlingly delicious mix will hold your attention. Traditionally served on crackers with drinks.

Preparation time: 25 minutes cooking or overnight soaking for salt fish + 15 minutes + 1 hour marinating. Serves 6–8

225 g/8 oz dried salt cod or herring, prepared (see page 39) or canned salt fish, drained thoroughly

1 onion, finely chopped

½ scotch bonnet or chilli pepper, de-seeded and finely chopped

2–3 tbsp finely chopped fresh parsley

1 sweet green pepper, de-seeded and finely chopped

2 firm tomatoes, finely chopped

For the dressing:

juice of 1 lime

2 tbsp olive or vegetable oil

freshly ground black pepper to taste

1.   Place the prepared salt fish in a glass or ceramic bowl with all the ingredients, except the tomatoes.

2.   Mix the dressing ingredients and add to the bowl. Mix well. Cover with cling film and place in the refrigerator overnight (ideally) If not, let sit refrigerated for about an hour so the flavours can get a chance to blend.

3.   Just before serving, add the tomatoes, and gently mix all the ingredients together. Serve with crackers or thin small rounds of toast.

Crispy Salty Nibbles

Home-made vegetable chips are delicious and are quite often fried up from cooked produce the day after. Sometimes baked in the oven (coconut slivers) or sunk deep into hot oil (sweet potatoes) they are best eaten immediately. Commercially made green banana and plantain chips are even more popular in the Caribbean than potato chips (crisps).

Fried Roasted Breadfruit

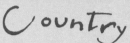

It was to secure a shipment of breadfruit plants for the West Indian colonies that Captain Bligh sailed the Bounty to the South Pacific in the first place. The famous story of the mutiny on the Bounty has been well documented and romanticised. Breadfruit, which is now a staple in the Caribbean, was finally brought from Tahiti to Jamaica by Captain Bligh in 1793 and from there this starchy fruit was introduced around the islands. It is a tall tree with large and beautiful five-pronged leaves. Breadfruit has a distinct aroma and a creamy flesh. It is seasonal and must be cooked before eating.

This snack is best made with second-day, or leftover roasted breadfruit.

Preparation and cooking time: 15 minutes + roasting breadfruit. Makes about 16 slices

1 roasted breadfruit (see page 160), peeled, cored and sliced into 1 cm/¹⁄₂-inch wedges

oil, for deep-frying

salt

1. Heat the oil in a large skillet and fry the breadfruit slices on each side until golden.
2. Remove and drain on kitchen paper. Sprinkle with salt while still warm and serve.

Cook's tip: This is really good cut into even smaller pieces and dipped in Lime Vinaigrette (see page 191).

APPETISERS: Teasers, Tantalisers & Nibbles · 48

Salt Fish Fritters

These bite-sized fritters – known as 'stamp and go', 'ackra' or affectionately as 'flittas' in Jamaica – are very similar to 'bacalaitos' from Puerto Rico but are much smaller.
Preparation time: 25 minutes cooking or overnight soaking for salt fish + 20 minutes + 20 minutes cooking. Makes about 24

225 g/8 oz salt fish, prepared (see page 39) and flaked, or canned bacalao, drained thoroughly
3 spring onions, chopped, use white and green parts
2 garlic cloves, finely chopped
1 large plum tomato, de-seeded and chopped finely
1/2 scotch bonnet pepper, de-seeded and chopped finely, or a few dashes of hot pepper sauce
1 tsp baking powder
175 g/3/4 cup plain flour
1 egg, beaten
60 ml/1/4 cup water
about 60 ml/1/4 cup oil, for shallow-frying

1. Mix the prepared salt fish with the rest of the finely chopped seasonings. Mix the baking powder with the flour and then add the salt fish mixture and mix together evenly. Stir in the beaten egg.
2. Little by little, add the milk or cold water until you have a lumpy batter.
3. Heat the oil in a large heavy bottomed skillet and add the annatto to colour it, if using.
4 . Drop batter by the spoonful into the skillet of hot oil. Fry and turn when just golden brown. Remove from pan with a slotted spatula and drain on kitchen paper to remove excess oil.

Cook's tip: Crab fritters are a more delicate fritter. Substitute for the salt fish 225 g/8 oz crabmeat, flaked.

Fritters are made with all kinds of variations. As you move around the islands you will find some batters are airier than others (use baking powder or beaten eggs). Some are made with grated tubers like sweet potato or yam instead of flour or cornmeal.

Savoury fritters can be served with or without dipping sauce, hot sauce or salsa: try Love Apple (Tomato) Sauce (see page 194) or a tomato coulis. All fritters are very moreish; be sure to serve them as soon as possible after frying as they will get soggy.

SALT MACKEREL
£1.25 PER L/B

Cornmeal Pumpkin Fritters

Jamaica

Two very popular ingredients used in the Caribbean are combined here. The texture of these is not as chewy as the other fritters and they are more substantial, due to the use of cornmeal. Very easy to make, tasty and satisfying, they make a good snack anytime. They are even better when served with a fresh tomato sauce such as Love Apple (Tomato) Sauce (page 194). *Preparation time: 15 minutes + 20 minutes cooking. Makes about 16 fritters*

130 g/¾ cup fine yellow cornmeal

50 g/½ cup plain flour

1 tsp baking powder

½ tsp ground cumin

1 cup coarsely grated pumpkin

1 spring onion, chopped finely

½ tsp finely chopped scotch bonnet pepper
   or chilli (optional)

1 egg, beaten

¼ cup water

salt and pepper

oil, for shallow-frying

1. Mix the dry ingredients in a bowl.
2. Add the pumpkin, spring onion and pepper or chilli and then fold in the egg and add water until the consistency is smooth and thick. (You might need a little more or less water.)
3. Heat the oil for frying until very hot.
4. Drop spoonfuls of batter into the hot oil and fry until golden all over. Drain on kitchen paper to remove excess oil. Serve right away.

'Bite & Kiss' (Jerk Shrimp with Soured Cream & Mango Salsa)

The jerk shrimp is scorchingly hot but you cool down immediately with the contrast of the soured cream mixture and the tangy salsa. The recipe was developed by Joseph Lamarca, an American chef who won an international jerk recipe competition for it. Dip the shrimp into the cream and then into the salsa, getting a bit of everything on your fork with each bite. I promise the shrimp will simply vanish!

Preparation time: 1 hour marinating + 10 minutes cooking + 20 minutes. Serves 6

For the shrimp:
1 kg/2 lb 4 oz jumbo raw prawns, peeled and de-veined
3 tbsp Jerk Seasoning (see page 127 or Walkerswood ready-made)
4 tbsp olive oil

For the salsa:
1 red pepper, de-seeded and diced
1 green pepper, de-seeded and diced
1 vidalia onion or other sweet onion, e.g red, chopped
1 celery stick, diced
1 firm mango, peeled, stoned and diced

For the salsa dressing:
60 ml/¼ cup olive oil
2 tbsp wine vinegar
salt and pepper

For the soured cream dip:
4 tbsp soured cream
4 tbsp mayonnaise
1 tbsp creamed horseradish
1 tsp lemon juice

1. Mix the prawns, jerk seasoning and oil together and set aside to marinate for 1 hour in the refrigerator.
2. While the shrimp is marinating make the salsa: combine all the diced ingredients together in a separate dish.
3. For the salsa dressing, mix all the ingredients and stir into the salsa ingredients.
4. For the dip, mix the soured cream, mayonnaise, horseradish and lemon juice together in a bowl and then chill until ready to use.
5. Preheat the grill to medium or light the barbecue.
6 . Grill the marinated shrimp in batches for 2 minutes on each side.
7. To serve, place the soured cream mixture in centre of a large platter (I usually use a large lettuce leaf instead of a bowl). Arrange the shrimp around the edge of the platter leaving space for a spoonful of the salsa in between.

Sticky Citrus Chicken Wings

These succulent wings are both sweet and tangy.
Preparation and cooking time: 1 hour marinating + 30 minutes. Makes 12 wings

12 chicken wings, jointed (discard tips)
For the seasoning:
1 tsp garlic powder
1/2 tsp dried thyme
1 tsp onion powder
1 tsp hot pepper sauce
salt and white pepper

For the sauce:
juice of 1 grapefruit
juice of 1 orange
juice of 1 lime
1 tbsp white vinegar
175 g/3/4 cup brown sugar
1 tsp ground cumin
1/2 scotch bonnet pepper, de-seeded and sliced
1 loosely packed tbsp grated orange zest

1. First of all prepare the chicken. Wash and pat dry. Season with the garlic, thyme, onion and hot sauce, rubbing the spices into the chicken pieces and adding salt and pepper to taste. Cover and refrigerate for an hour to marinate.

2. Meanwhile, strain the fresh juices (they should be about 225 ml/1 cup in total) into a non-stick pan and add all the other ingredients with the exception of the orange zest. Heat until the sauce bubbles and thickens. This will take about 30 minutes. At the very end of cooking, add the zest.

3. Light the barbecue or preheat the grill. Or preheat the oven to 180°C/350°F/Gas Mark 4.

4. Put the chicken pieces on an oiled baking sheet or grill rack and brush with oil if you think it necessary. Cook for 25–30 minutes, or until the juices run clear when the thickest part is pierced with a fine skewer. Drain off excess oil on kitchen paper.

5. Coat the chicken with sauce and serve immediately. Or put the sauce in a bowl and serve with the chicken as a dip.

Amuse-bouche literally means 'amuseing the mouth'. This is a terrific way of eating and it fits to a clove head the introduction of a new recipe or cuisine. Here, restaurants prepare lots of little platefuls of food so anyone can try a little bit of this or that without a serious commitment. The Chinese do it with dim sum so why not do it with Caribbean!

Coco Fish Cakes

Traditional fish cakes are a very comforting kind of dish but there is no reason they can't be made a little more exciting. These cakes are unique because instead of using the traditional potato we use boiled coco (eddoe) which has a delicate, nutty flavour and holds up with our zappy island seasonings. Substitute other tubers, such as yam, cassava or potatoes, if coco is not available.

Preparation time: 1 hour + 20 minutes cooking. Makes 10 medium-size or 20 party-size fish cakes

450 g/1 lb coco, peeled and cut up

1 tbsp butter

350 g/12 oz cooked fish fillets, e.g. snapper, tilapia or other flaky fish

1 onion, finely chopped

2 spring onions, finely chopped

½ scotch bonnet pepper, de-seeded and finely chopped, or a dash of hot pepper sauce

¼ teaspoon grated nutmeg

1 tbsp finely chopped fresh coriander or parsley

2 tbsp snipped fresh chives

3 eggs

salt and pepper

about 200 g/2 cups breadcrumbs, for coating

oil, for frying

To serve:

lime wedges

Red Pepper Jelly (see page 197)

salt and pepper to taste

1. Boil the yam chunks in boiling, salted water until tender, about 20 minutes, depending on the size of the chunks.
2. Mash the drained cocos with the butter and allow to cool.
3. Mix in the fish, onion, spring onion, hot pepper, nutmeg, coriander or parsley and chives. Season with salt and pepper. Stir in one of the eggs and mix thoroughly.
4. With floured hands, form into cakes. Place on a baking sheet and chill in the fridge for half an hour.
5. Beat the remaining eggs. Dip each fish cake in the egg and then roll in the breadcrumbs.
6. Heat the oil in a deep-sided frying pan over moderate heat and, when hot, add the fish cakes. Fry for about 5 minutes on each side or until golden.
7. Serve hot or cold, with wedges of lime and a spoonful of the pepper jelly.

Cook's tip: These fish cakes are very versatile. They can be made with almost any fish or a mixture of salt cod and fresh fish. To make them even more special, add a large handful of peeled cooked prawns to the fish mixture.

Jerk Lamb Kebabs with Guava Dip

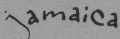
Jamaica

This non-traditional use of jerk is great for a cocktail party. I like to present just one piece of meat on a long wooden skewer, served with guava dipping sauce on the side. It is a bit extravagant but if you have bought a good cut of lamb your guests will appreciate the elegance.

Preparation time: 1 hour marinating + 10 minutes cooking + making guava sauce. Makes about 12–18 pieces

1.4 kg/3 lb boneless leg of lamb cut into 4 cm/1½-inch cubes
2–3 tbsp Jerk Seasoning (see page 127 or Walkerswood ready-made)
1 tbsp oil
Fiery Guava Dipping Sauce (see page 190), to serve

1. Place the cubes of lamb in a glass bowl and rub thoroughly with the jerk seasoning and oil. Cover and refrigerate for at least 1 hour.
2. Grill the meat either on a griddle pan or under the grill. Or you can thread several on a skewer and place on a barbecue. Cook slowly to your liking – rare, well done or medium rare. Turn once or twice and don't allow to burn.
3. Serve warm with the guava sauce.

Cook's tips: If grilling on wooden skewers, soak them in water for about 20 minutes before using.

Soups

COOLING, WARMING & COMFORTING BOWLS

There are as many soups as there are ingredients and many of them are associated with particular occasions. 'Saturday soup' is a clearinghouse for the end of the week when we are always so busy fixing house and repairing ourselves. It is a one-pot lunchtime affair quite often made with beef and substantial amounts of vegetables and 'blue food' or 'hard food' (yam, dumpling and potato).

'Mannish water' or 'goat head soup' is prepared for most serious occasions in Jamaica, where a goat is usually slaughtered for the feast. Christenings, ground-breakings, weddings, wakes and all-night sessions are all occasions for this soup. Virtually nothing of the goat is left out and it is a potion with claims to aphrodisiac qualities. If this is at all possible, mannish water could be considered a masculine soup: it is often cooked by men and is more likely than not to be cooked on an open fire, outdoors.

The heartiness of our soup defies the image of light meals in the heat of the tropics. Truth is, soup is quite often the main meal and, in order to be satisfying, a lot of our traditional soups are filled with meat, vegetables, beans and ground provisions, noodles or dumplings. The soup base is usually meat, chicken or fish stock and the consistency can run from a broth to a rib-sticking gumbo.

Chilled Cucumber Soup

Cold soups are not hugely popular in the Caribbean and truthfully you will most likely run into them in upscale restaurants or private homes. I can't imagine why they aren't enjoyed more often as they are cooling, delicious and simple to make. Cucumbers are available everywhere in the Caribbean.

Preparation time: 20 minutes + 30 minutes chilling time. Serves 4

2 cucumbers, de-seeded and peeled (leave half the skin on one for a little colour)

500 ml/2 cups chicken stock

½ onion, chopped

225 ml/1 cup natural yogurt, plus extra to serve

75 g/½ cup fresh white breadcrumbs or 2 slices of white bread

2 tbsp fresh single cream

1–2 tsps lime or lemon juice

½ scotch bonnet pepper, de-seeded and minced (optional)

salt and white pepper

a dash of Pepper Sherry (see page 195) or regular dry sherry, to serve

fresh mint leaves, to garnish

1. Blend all the ingredients in a food processor until it has the consistency of a gazpacho.
2. Chill the soup in the freezer for about 30 minutes, so that it is almost icy when served.
3. Add the sherry. You can top with a swirl of yogurt and a mint leaf.

Cook's tip: A tasty addition to this soup is a spoonful or two of Solomon Gundy (see page 45). It might be preferable to use vegetable or fish stock rather than chicken, if you decide to jazz this soup up with the mysterious and flavourful gundy.

A travel story We went to see the leatherback turtles performing their annual egg-laying ritual on the beach at Grande Riviere on the north coast of Trinidad. It is a protected environment (no turtle soup here) and off the beaten track. The event began as we sat on the edge of absolute darkness, listening to the sea relentlessly washing the shoreline. Only candlelight lit the tables, which had earlier been delicately bejeweled with pink petals and freshly picked fern leaves by 'Tutankamen', the tall and dedicated table decorator working the hotel.

I was carefree and barefoot on the sandy gazebo floor and anxious for the event to begin but Piero, the owner of Mon Plaisir where we were staying, had made a special order for our supper and held us captive. He presented us with the most outstanding fish soup I ever had. It exemplified the wealth of flavour that can be captured in a delicately seasoned fish broth and he demonstrated that it is possible to serve this with green banana, potato and chayote as a 'light' first course. Both the meal and the company were so good that we did not see the turtles until hours later. It was an incredibly moving experience and I had no imagination left for what I was going to witness, but that's a whole other story.

Caribbean Fish Tea

Any hot edible liquid is called 'tea' in the Caribbean, including fish broth. This can also be made with fish heads and bones instead of whole fish but the addition of some of the flesh makes it into a more substantial dish. This is the soup that so impressed me at Grande Riviere in Trinidad (see opposite).

Preparation time: 15 minutes + 30 minutes for stock + 25 minutes cooking. Serves 6

1 kg/2 lb 4 oz juicy fresh fish, e.g. red snapper, grouper or bream

300 ml/½ pint dry white wine

110 g/4 oz chopped onion

110 g/4 oz chopped carrot

1 tsp black peppercorns

1 tsp salt

2 fresh bay leaves (or 1 dried)

3 thyme sprigs

½ tsp sugar

2 scotch bonnet peppers

1.2 litres/2 pints water

4 small green bananas, peeled and sliced

2 tomatoes, peeled, de-seeded and chopped

650g/1½ lb selection of ground provisions, e.g. yam, breadfruit or eddoes, cut into cubes

chopped fresh parsley, chandon beni or coriander or snipped fresh chives, to garnish

1. To make the broth, place the fish, white wine, onion, carrot, peppercorns, salt, bay leaves, thyme, sugar, hot pepper and water in a large pot and bring to the boil. Reduce the heat to low, cover the pot and cook for 30 minutes. Be careful not to pierce the hot pepper at any point.

2. Remove from the heat and allow to cool a little. Then strain the stock through a fine sieve or muslin into a clean pan. Remove the flesh of the fish from the bones and return to the stock.

3. Add the new hot pepper, green bananas, tomatoes and ground provisions to the stock, again being careful not to pierce the pepper. Bring to the boil and then lower the heat and simmer for 15 minutes, or until the green bananas and other vegetables are tender. Remove the pepper. Taste and adjust the seasoning. Serve sprinkled with fresh herbs.

Pumpkin Lobster Bisque

Embodying the flavours of the Caribbean, this gloriously decadent soup is the perfect introduction to a Caribbean feast. 'Calabaza', the Spanish name for pumpkin, is common throughout the islands and a thick, rich pumpkin soup is just as widespread.

Preparation and cooking time: about 1 hour. Serves 6

1 litre/1¾ pints vegetable or chicken stock

1 lobster tail

50 g/2 oz butter

1 large onion, finely chopped

2 garlic cloves, crushed

1 kg/2 lb 4 oz pumpkin or butternut squash, peeled, de-seeded and chopped coarsely

4 plum tomatoes, peeled de-seeded and chopped

1 fresh thyme sprig

1 scotch bonnet pepper or ½ tsp hot pepper sauce (optional)

125 ml/½ cup single cream or full-cream milk

a few dashes of Pepper Sherry (see page 197) or sweet sherry

oil, for brushing

salt and ground white pepper

1 tbsp finely chopped fresh coriander, to garnish

1. Pour 500 ml/2 cups of the stock into a medium-sized saucepan and bring to the boil. Add the lobster tail and simmer for 15 minutes.

2. Remove the lobster tail from the pan and set aside to cool a little. Then remove the meat from the shell. Reserve the stock and the lobster meat.

3. In a large saucepan, heat the butter over gentle heat, add the onion and garlic and sauté for 5 minutes. Stir in the pumpkin and cook for about 10–15 minutes, or until it is soft.

4. Add the tomatoes, thyme and the whole scotch bonnet pepper (if using) and pour in all the remaining stock. Bring back to the boil, lower the heat again and simmer for 20 minutes.

5. Remove the pan from the heat. Take out the hot pepper and thyme and discard. Liquidise the soup in a food processor or liquidiser, being careful not to make it too smooth. Alternatively, using a hand-held blender or potato masher, mash the ingredients in the pan.

6. Return the soup to the pan and heat gently. If you have not used a scotch bonnet pepper and wish to add some heat to the soup, now add the pepper sauce, then the cream or milk and sherry. Check and adjust the seasoning.

7. Finally, slice the lobster meat into slices and brush with a little oil. Heat a griddle pan or non-stick frying pan and flash-grill the lobster slices.

8. To serve, ladle the soup into the bowls, place a slice of lobster in each bowl and sprinkle on the coriander.

Cook's tip: If you don't mind spending a little more time on this soup, you might try roasting the pumpkin first. That really brings out its sweet, nutty flavour.

Hot & Sour Seafood Soup

Here's a tribute to the Asian influence in Caribbean food, whose presence assures the availability of Chinese ingredients. Pak choy is easily available in the Caribbean and we eat it mostly steamed as a vegetable side dish as an alternative to cabbage. The same goes with mustard greens.

Preparation and cooking time: 25 minutes. Serves 4

1 litres/1¾ cups fish stock

1 tilapia or other medium-sized white fish fillet, cut into pieces

4 scallops (optional)

3 pak choy leaves or other 'Chinese' greens

1 spring onion, chopped

4 jumbo prawns

4 tbsp cane vinegar or distilled (white) malt vinegar

2 tsp oyster sauce

¼ tsp hot pepper sauce

soya sauce or salt to taste

1.   In a large pot, bring the fish stock to a boil. Add the fish, scallops and pak choy, reduce the heat and simmer for 4 minutes.

2.   Add the spring onion and prawns and cook a further 2 minutes.

3.   Stir in the vinegar and oyster and pepper sauce. Check the seasoning, adding a dash of soy sauce or salt if necessary. Remove from heat and divide the fish and greens amongst four bowls. Add the liquid and serve at once.

Cook's tip: Just about any delicious seafood will work with this dish, so long as it has a short cooking time.

Quick-time Pepperpot Soup – a 'Saturday Soup'

Jamaica

This is the fast version, leaving out the pig's tail, salt beef and dumplings. The key here is to use a good beef stock and try to find some 'ground provisions'. This soup is characteristically a Jamaican tradition, the main ingredient being callaloo greens. Made the traditional way it is hearty and filling with its cocos (eddoes), yellow yam, dumplings and meats. The traditional way takes a few hours to cook because of the pig's tail and stewing beef, and probably dates back to a basic stew made by our native Tainos. It has been africanised, anglicised and everyone else seems to have done their version of it.

The dish called 'callaloo' in Trinidad is a similar soup, but it contains dasheen and tannia leaves. Using the same salted meats and sometimes crab, it tends to be thicker than ours. In St Lucia there is a stew called 'callaloo' which is even heartier, with lamb, chicken, beef, pumpkin and green bananas. The common denominator for all these recipes is the use of leafly greens.

Notably though, the Amerindian 'pepperpot' of Guyana is not a soup. It is a never-ending stew, which can be kept on the fire for generations, with food added daily. It is kept safe by the addition of 'cassareep', a sticky black liquid made from an extract of cassava, which preserves meat.

Preparation time: 20 minutes for preparing fresh callaloo and yams + 30 minutes cooking. Serves 6

4 cocos (eddoes) peeled and cut in 1 cm/$\frac{1}{2}$-inch cubes

225 g/8 oz yellow yam, peeled and cut in 1 cm/$\frac{1}{2}$-inch cubes

2 tbsp butter

1 onion chopped

3 spring onions, chopped

2 garlic cloves, chopped

1 tablespoon fresh thyme leaves

8–10 okras, sliced

6 allspice berries or $\frac{1}{2}$ tsp ground allspice

675 g/1$\frac{1}{2}$ lb fresh callaloo leaves or 2 x 19 oz cans
(or spinach equivalent)

225 ml/1 cup coconut milk

2 litres/3$\frac{1}{2}$ pints beef stock

salt and pepper

1 whole scotch bonnet pepper

1. Boil some water in a saucepan and cook the coco and yam pieces until just tender (10–15 minutes). Drain.
2. Melt the butter in a large soup pot. Add the onion, spring onion, garlic, okras, thyme and allspice and sauté, stirring gently, until soft. Add the calaloo and stir in the coconut milk. Cook for 5 minutes or until the calaloo is soft (if using fresh).
3. Add the stock and bring to the boil. Simmer for 5 minutes and then purée the soup with a hand blender. (This step is optional and, if you don't want a blended soup, the pepper, coco and yam can be boiled together with the stock).
4. After blending, add the scotch bonnet, the coco and yam and return to the boil. Adjust the salt and pepper to taste. Simmer for 10 minutes more. Just before finishing, remove the pepper and pimento berries (if using).
5. Serve hot, making sure to divide the coco and yam between the bowls.

Cook's tips: Please don't allow the whole scotch bonnet to burst when stirring the pot or it will be very hot. If you prefer, you can use vegetable, chicken or seafood instead of the beef stock.

Red 'Peas' Soup

Jamaica

This soup is an easy version, made without the traditional Jamaican pig's tail or beef. But it does have the option for chewy 'spinners' (dumplings) and all the spices.

Preparation time: soaking overnight + 20 minutes + 2½ hours cooking. Serves 6–8

For the spinners:

75 g/½ cup plain flour

a pinch of salt

For the soup:

2.85 litres/5 pints vegetable, chicken or beef stock

400 g/14 oz dried red beans, soaked overnight and rinsed

250 ml/1 cup coconut milk

1 scotch bonnet pepper

a dash of hot pepper sauce

2 fresh thyme sprigs

3 spring onions

4 garlic cloves

10 allspice berries or 1 tsp ground allspice

450 g/1 lb coco or yam and sweet potato, peeled and cut into 2.5 cm/1-inch pieces

salt and pepper

1. Fill a large pot with 2.4 litres/½ gallon of stock. Add the beans and bring to the boil. Lower the heat and cook for about 1½ hours.

2. Prepare the spinners: mix the flour and salt together and then add enough water to make a stiff dough. Pinch small pieces off (about the size of a wine cork). Roll them into 'snakes' about 7.5 cm/3 inches long. Set aside.

3. Add the coconut milk and seasonings to the soup and cook for a further half-hour before adding the coco or yam, sweet potato and spinners.

4. Cook for another half-hour or so and reduce heat to a simmer. If it is getting thick, top up with the remaining stock. The beans and vegetables should be tender and the soup a little thick, like pea soup should be. Taste and adjust the salt and pepper if necessary. Take out the spring onions, thyme and scotch bonnet pepper and serve, making sure that everyone gets a share of all the bits and pieces.

Cook's tip: You can add up to 900 g/2 lb meat (salt beef and/or pig's tail) or chicken if you wish. This should be boiled along with the beans.

Spicy Orange Soup with Chicken Won Tons

This soup is light, quick and flavourful and not at all traditional but the blend of spices will taste familiar.
Preparation time: 15 minutes + about 30 minutes cooking. Serves 6

For the won tons:

225 g/8 oz chicken mince

½ tsp ground cinnamon

1 tsp finely chopped or grated fresh root ginger

½ tsp ground cumin

½ tsp salt

¼ tsp ground white pepper

1 spring onion, chopped

24 won ton wrappers

For the soup:

1 litre/1¾ pints chicken broth

juice of 2 oranges, strained

1 tsp sugar

1 tsp butter

1 scotch bonnet pepper, left whole (no heat just flavour)

1 tbsp Pepper Sherry (see page 195) or sweet sherry

1 tsp grated orange zest

green top of a spring onion sliced finely diagonally, to garnish

1. Season the mince with the spices, salt and pepper and spring onion. Form into about 24 balls, 1 tsp each.
2. Place each ball in the centre of a won ton wrapper, dampen the edges with a touch of water and pinch together at the top.
3. Mix the broth with the orange juice, sugar and butter and bring to the boil. Drop in the whole pepper and simmer for 3 minutes (this gives flavour but no heat). Drop in the chicken won tons and simmer for about 15–20 minutes, until cooked through.
4. Check broth and add salt to taste. Add the sherry, simmer for a further minute and then turn off the heat. Discard the pepper. Stir in the orange zest.
5. Serve hot in bowls with the won tons distributed evenly and sprinkle with spring onion tops.

Cook's tip: This can be made very successfully without the won ton wrappers. Just roll the chicken into balls and drop into the soup as described. If you do this, you might want to make the balls a little larger and therefore only make 12 of them.

SIDE SALADS, CRUNCHY LUNCHES & LIGHT BITES

In this section I have selected salad dishes that can be eaten either on the side or as complete meals in themselves. Some incorporate both raw and cooked items.

Traditionally, in the Caribbean, green salad was not a big item on the menu. Pickled beets, hot pickled cucumbers and slices of avocado were all served, particularly on buffets, but usually considered condiments or side dishes. The word 'salad' in Jamaica sometimes referred strictly to tomatoes. Today, versions of coleslaw and 'tossed salad' are popular everywhere.

All the ingredients exist in the Caribbean for the 'big salad' as a light meal option and the demand has certainly grown. This is an area where tradition has given way to contemporary style and you will find all kinds of vegetarian or seafood, meat and pasta salads on the islands. With the impact of this healthier trend, far more non-traditional salad items are being grown and imported and you will find quite a range in the better supermarkets.

The best seafood salads can be found where the yachting and sport-fishing crowds gather, like in the Bahamas, Virgin and Cayman Islands, Barbados or in better restaurants throughout the Caribbean.

Take advantage of all the limes, sour oranges and other citrus fruit to squeeze abundant flavour over your salads. Your tongue will be thrilled and there is barely a calorie to be found. See Conch Salad (page 78) and the Jerked Chicken with Avocado and Papaya Salad (page 85) for examples of how to do this.

Warm Cabbage Salad with Pineapple and Peanuts

This dish won't take much time and, if everything is fresh and lightly cooked, I suspect that it's even good for you. Green cabbage is a standard food throughout the islands and is used in salads and rundowns, fried with salt fish or steamed with carrots. The chances are you'll eat cabbage at least once a week in the Caribbean.

Preparation and cooking time: 20 minutes. Serves 4 (as a side dish)

oil, for frying

350 g/12 oz peeled fresh pineapple, cored and cut into chunks

1 onion, chopped into wedges

3–4 tsp finely chopped fresh rosemary or thyme

2 tbsp roasted peanuts

1 tsp honey (only necessary if the pineapple is too tart)

350 g/12 oz green cabbage, chopped

salt and pepper

1. Heat about a tbsp of oil in a large skillet. Add the pineapple chunks to the hot oil, stirring so they don't burn (you do want the pineapple to brown slightly).

2. Add the onion, herbs and peanuts and fry for 2 more minutes. Taste the pineapple and add the honey if you need to at this time.

3. Toss in the cabbage and sprinkle on a little salt and pepper. Stir for about 4–6 minutes until the cabbage is lightly cooked. Then serve with rice.

Smoked Marlin Salad

Smoked marlin is the Caribbean's answer to smoked salmon. Its pale flesh retains a delicate quality after smoking. If you are unable to find marlin, use smoked halibut or tuna instead. You'll need very thinly sliced smoked fish, ready prepared.

Preparation time: 10 minutes + making sauce and pepper jelly. Serves 2

110 g/4 oz green salad leaves

2 tbsp olive oil

1 tbsp vinegar

6 slices of smoked marlin

1 small ripe avocado, peeled and sliced

salt and freshly ground pepper

To serve:

75 ml/generous ¼ cup Creamy Lime Sauce (see page 188)

2 tbsp Red Pepper Jelly (see page 197 or ready-made)

To garnish:

1 tbsp capers

1 onion, sliced thinly and separated into rings

1. Toss the greens with the oil, vinegar, salt and pepper. Place on two plates.
2. Arrange 3 slices of fish and 3 slices of avocado, alternately, beside the salad.
3. Garnish with a dollop (about 1 tbsp) of lime sauce and 2 tsp of pepper jelly on either side of the fish.
4. Sprinkle the capers and onion rings on top and then dress with freshly ground black pepper.

Christophene & Cantaloupe Salad

Traditionally, christophenes are cooked but prepared raw they are a clean and crunchy addition to salads.
Preparation time: 15 minutes + making dressing. Serves 4–6

2 christophenes, peeled, cored, sliced

½ cantaloupe melon, peeled and sliced

1 shallot, sliced in thin rings

225 g/8 oz rocket or watercress, stems removed

1 tbsp chopped mixed fresh herbs, e.g. oregano, coriander, tarragon and/or parsley

Lime Vinaigrette or Guava Vinaigrette (see page 191 or 192), to serve

1. Toss all ingredients together with the dressing and serve at once.

Cook's tip: Add seedless grapes, cut in half, if you wish more sweetness in the salad.

Fancy Coleslaw

Coleslaw with cabbage and carrot is a Caribbean standard. This version is made with the addition of shredded fresh coconut, sweet tangy pineapple and that spike of hot pepper which altogether makes it special.
Preparation time: 30 minutes + chilling. Serves 6–8

125 g/1 cup shredded white or red cabbage

125 g/1 cup shredded carrots

75 g/½ cup shredded fresh coconut

1 onion, chopped finely or shredded

75 g/½ cup chopped pineapple

2 tbsp golden raisins

½ tsp de-seeded and minced scotch bonnet pepper (optional)

For the dressing:

2 tbsp brown sugar

1 tbsp white vinegar

about 250 g/1 cup mayonnaise (you can use more or less, according to your taste)

1. To make the dressing, mix the sugar and vinegar together and then add the mayonnaise and mix well.
2. Toss all the ingredients together and chill before serving.

Cook's tip: It stays crunchy in the refrigerator and actually tastes better after a few hours, so can be made a day ahead.

Green Banana & Salt Fish Salad

Many Spanish and English-speaking islands make a similar salad to this, sometimes using mayonnaise instead of oil. Green bananas, referred to as 'figs' on some islands, are quite starchy and bland and must be cooked, usually boiled. This dish can easily be adapted for a vegetarian meal if you leave out the salt fish.

Preparation and cooking time: 1 hour + 30 minutes cooling. Serves 6–8

2 tbsp cane vinegar or distilled (white) malt vinegar

8 small green bananas, topped and tailed and slit down one side

125 g/4½ oz prepared salt fish

1 onion, sliced in rings

1 spring onion, chopped

70 g/¼ cup stuffed green olives, sliced, or capers

For the dressing:

1 garlic clove, crushed

½ scotch bonnet pepper, de-seeded and chopped finely

1 tsp Dijon mustard

1 tsp sugar

juice of 1 lime

70 ml/¼ cup olive oil

1 ripe avocado, peeled, stoned and chopped (optional)

freshly ground black pepper

salt (optional)

1.   Drop one tbsp of vinegar into a large pot of salted water. (This prevents the blackening of bananas and the pot. It is best to use a non-reactive pan.) When the water boils, add the bananas. Cook for 20 minutes, or until tender.

2.   Meanwhile, prepare the salt fish (see page 39).

3.   Drain the bananas and leave until cool enough to handle. Peel away the skin and cut into 1.5 cm /⅝-inch slices. Place in a large bowl.

4.   Add the fish, onion, spring onion and olives. Whisk together all the dressing ingredients and then toss everything together. Sprinkle with black pepper and salt to taste, chill for at least an hour before serving so that flavours can blend and develop. Toss in the avocado (if using) just before serving; a squeeze of lime or lemon juice will prevent it from darkening.

Cook's tip: Try using a boiled breadfruit instead of bananas. 'Gros Michel' bananas are the nicest.

Conch Salad 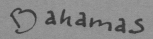 Bahamas

A Bahamian speciality, conch (pronounced 'conk') is eaten both raw and cooked, throughout the islands. Best identified by its large pink shell, the meat in it is used in many ways, including soups, fritters and curries. It is known as 'lambie' on the French islands where it is also cooked in rice or with beans.

Conch is very chewy and benefits from both pounding and lime juice as ways of tenderising. The lime juice virtually cooks the conch in this salad, using the same principle as in a 'ceviche' (raw fish salad). When purchased commercially conch has usually been prepared (the tough outer skin has been removed). Its sweetish seafood flavour is quite distinct.
Preparation time: 20 minutes + 30 minutes marinating. Serves 4–6

400 g/2 cups (about 4) finely chopped (minced) conch meat
1 small Bermuda, vidalia or other sweet onion, minced
2 tomatoes, de-seeded and finely chopped
¼ cup finely chopped celery or green pepper
½ scotch bonnet pepper, de-seeded and minced
juice of 1 lime
1 tsp cane vinegar or distilled (white) malt vinegar
salt and pepper
chopped fresh parsley, to garnish

1. Mix all the ingredients together and allow to sit for at least 30 minutes before serving.

Cook's tip: The salad can be chilled for a few hours but don't add tomatoes immediately if keeping refrigerated overnight.

Warm Green Gungo, Red Pea & Broad Bean Salad, with Roasted Pumpkin Seeds

Jamaica

The fresh green gungo pea season starts around November and if it wasn't so warm we'd call it a winter crop. Most people in Jamaica take advantage by switching from 'rice and peas' made with red kidney beans to 'gungo rice and peas' for the holiday festivities. Gungo, which is a big favourite, is often cooked in coconut milk and made into stews and soups.

Since you can get all three peas and beans fresh at this time, try this salad as a side dish. The 'pepitas' or shelled pumpkin seeds add crunch if you give them a little toasting first. Stand by though, as they'll start 'popping' in the pan and are ready after a very short time.

This is also nice cold, served on rocket leaves. You can also use the Lime or Coriander Vinaigrette Dressings (see page 191) if you prefer.

Preparation time: dressing 10 minutes + 35 minutes cooking. Serves 4–6

300 g/2 cups fresh broad beans	1 tbsp balsamic vinegar
200 g/1 cup fresh green gungo peas	60 ml/¼ cup olive oil
200 g/1 cup fresh red beans	1 tbsp chopped fresh dill
For the dressing:	2 tbsp chopped fresh parsley
1 garlic clove, crushed	salt and pepper
1 tsp Dijon mustard	2 tablespoons 'pepitas' (shelled pumpkin seeds),
1 tsp sugar	to garnish

1. Boil the beans and peas in salted water for about 30 minutes or until tender. Drain.
2. While the peas are boiling, make the dressing by mixing all the ingredients in a large bowl. Season to taste with pepper and a pinch of salt.
3. Toast the pumpkin seeds carefully in a dry frying pan, being careful not to let them burn.
4. As soon as the peas are ready, drain them in a colander and then toss with the dressing. Sprinkle over the seeds and serve warm.

Grilled Lobster with Nutty Rice Salad

The Caribbean lobster is spiny and does not have those big claws found on most cold-water species. The height of lobster season brings about a rush of old recipes and some new dishes. My favourite lobster was freshly grilled on the beach in Cuba, with a little butter, salt, pepper and a squeeze of lime, very simple.

Preparation and cooking time: 45 minutes. Serves 2

2 x 225 g/8 oz lobster tails

1 garlic clove, very finely chopped

110g/½ cup white long-grain rice

180 ml/⅔ cup Creamy Coconut Dressing with Angostura Bitters or Lime or Coriander Vinaigrette (see page 188 or 191)

1 tsp butter, melted

2 tablespoons cashew nuts, roasted and broken up

2 tbsp finely chopped fresh parsley

2 handfuls mixed lettuce, torn into small pieces

salt and pepper

1 lime, quartered, to garnish

1. Season the lobster meat with salt, pepper and garlic. Chill until ready to grill.

2 . Cook the rice according to directions and allow it to cool.

3. Prepare the salad dressing of your choice and set aside in the refrigerator.

4. When the rice is ready, brush each lobster tail with butter melted and place on a greased pan under a hot grill for about 8–10 minutes.

5. Place the rice in a bowl and add the bashed-up cashew nuts, parsley and about 4 tbsp of salad dressing. Mix together. Then pack tightly in two 125 ml/½-cup bowls and invert on to the serving plates (or just spoon out loose if you wish).

6. When the lobster is ready, slice into pieces and place on top of rice. Surround with lettuce. Sprinkle lobster and lettuce with more dressing. Serve at room temperature, with lime wedges.

Cook's tip: Since we need to be vigilant about protecting the lobster during the breeding season, I would recommend that you use shrimp or other seafood for this salad whenever you can't find lobster. Calamari (squid) is also a good choice and can be prepared in a similar way. Both will take less time to cook than lobster tail.

Two-Potato Salad with Red Beans

I couldn't have a section on salads without including the ubiquitous potato salad – with a twist. Try to use waxy potatoes and look out for unusual varieties. I once found some little purple sweet potatoes for this and they were really pretty in the mix.
Preparation and cooking time: 30 minutes + 2 hours cooling and chilling. Serves 6

450 g/1 lb sweet potato
450 g/1 lb waxy potatoes, e.g. red-skinned
2 eggs (optional)
125 ml/½ cup mayonnaise
1 tbsp white wine vinegar
3 tsp Dijon mustard
1–2 garlic cloves, pressed
1 onion, grated or finely chopped
110 g/4 oz cooked or canned red kidney beans, or gungo beans
1 tsp salt
freshly ground black pepper
2 tbsp chopped fresh herbs, e.g. coriander, tarragon, dill and/or parsley

1. Peel the sweet potatoes and just wash the regular ones. Boil them together in a pan of salted water for about 20–25 minutes or until just tender. Check the sweet potatoes after 15 minutes as they may cook faster than the regular potatoes. If ready remove them with a slotted spoon whilst the others continue cooking. (You don't want any of them to be overcooked or they will fall apart.)
2. Meanwhile, hard-boil the eggs, if using, and then shell and chop them.
3. Mix the mayonnaise with vinegar, mustard, garlic and onion.
4. Drain the potatoes in a colander and peel the red ones while still warm. Cut all potatoes into bite-sized cubes. Dress with the mayonnaise mixture while still warm. Add the beans and egg if using and toss together with salt and pepper. On the last turn, add some of the chopped herbs, leaving some as a final green garnish.
5. Allow to cool and then keep in the refrigerator until ready to serve. This will give the flavours a chance to develop and become absorbed by the potatoes.
6. Serve sprinkled with the remaining herbs.

Escoveitched Chicken Salad

Tangy escoveitch brings a huge taste bite to this dish. Keeping in mind that many of us are watching our waistlines and our diets, you will be glad to know that this dish is relatively low in fat and calories.

Preparation and cooking time: 1 hour marinating + making sauce + 15 minutes. Serves 4

4 boneless, skinless chicken breasts

1 garlic clove, finely chopped

1 tbsp chopped fresh thyme

1 tbsp olive or vegetable oil

125 ml/½ cup Escoveitch Pickle Sauce (see page 195) or use ready-made

225 g/8 oz mixed salad leaves

tomatoes and cucumber, sliced

salt and pepper

best-quality extra-virgin olive oil, to serve (optional)

1. Wash the chicken and season with the salt, pepper garlic and thyme. Let marinate for at least an hour if you can. Meanwhile, make the sauce.

2. To cook the chicken, brush the breasts lightly with oil and then grill them whole, turning so they brown on both sides until cooked through (about 10 minutes). Slice.

3. Place the chicken in a bowl and marinate with most of the escoveitch sauce for 10 minutes or so.

4. Arrange the salad ingredients on a platter. Place the slices or strips of chicken on top. Sprinkle over a little more of the escoveitch sauce, top with some of the pickled vegetables pieces from the sauce and sprinkle over a little olive oil if you wish. Serve at room temperature or chilled, as preferred.

Cook's tip: Grilled fish strips or shrimp are just as delicious if you want an alternative to the chicken.

Jerked Chicken with Avocado and Papaya Salad

This dish can be made with leftover jerk chicken; chicken breasts can be substituted for thighs but won't be quite as succulent. It is spicy but not really hot because the fruity dressing and salad keep everything balanced.
Preparation and cooking time: 12 hours marinating + making Guava Vinaigrette + 20 minutes. Serves 4

For the chicken:

8 boneless chicken thighs, skin left on

salt or lime juice

1 tbsp Jerk Seasoning (see page 000 or Walkerswood ready-made)

1 tbsp oil

For the avocado and papaya salad:

1 small avocado, peeled and cut into small chunks

1 just-ripe papaya, peeled and cut into small chunks

1 spring onion, chopped finely

juice of 1 lime

salt and pepper

For the green salad:

225 g/8 oz mixed green lettuce leaves, torn into pieces

120 ml/½ cup Guava Vinaigrette (see page 190)

1 tbsp chopped fresh parsley, to garnish

1. Wash the chicken with either salt or juice of a lime. Pat dry and rub with jerk seasoning and oil. Leave in the refrigerator for an hour or two.

2. Light the barbecue or preheat a grill pan or grill. Cook the chicken for about 5 minutes on either side or until done. Allow to cool and then cut into strips, removing the skin if you prefer.

3. Mix the avocado and papaya with the spring onion, lime juice, salt and pepper.

4. Prepare the lettuce and divide between four plates. Layer each with chicken, and then top with avocado mixture. Dress with guava vinaigrette and garnish everything with parsley. It's best eaten at room temperature.

SCRUMPTIOUS SEASIDE SELECTION

One would expect the Caribbean islands to be saturated with seafood. The fact is that once you have left the coastline fresh fish can be hard to find and much of it is snatched up by the hotels and restaurants. Those of us who live inland have often relied more on salted cod, mackerel and shad as staples rather than on fresh fish and this is probably due to the days when refrigeration was an issue. Naturally, you can take home a fish to cook but supermarkets often freeze them and a great deal is lost in the process.

Nonetheless, you will easily find excellent fish and shellfish on most restaurant menus and it will be available fresh or even cooked on the roadside if you are on the coast. Keep in mind that a good curried lobster dinner is hard to beat.

Ackee & Salt Fish

Jamaica

This beloved recipe is unique to Jamaica; as a matter of fact it is considered our national dish. Ackees came to Jamaica from West Africa but in most of the countries where they grow they are not eaten. Ackee is a fruit encased in a bright orange pod with three large black seeds. Only the yellow flesh is eaten, as a vegetable. Waxy when raw, ackee becomes extremely soft and delicate when boiled. The slightly nutty flavour and silky texture can only be likened to avocado but it really has to be tasted to be appreciated. Ackees can be curried or baked in patties or pastry.

Ackees are seasonal, so canned ackees can be used. This dish is delicious with Roasted Breadfruit (see page 180), Fried Ripe Plantains (see page 171) and plain rice.

Preparation and cooking time: 45 minutes. Serves 6

1 kg/2 lb 2 oz salt cod (prepared)

2 tbsp cooking oil (coconut oil is ideal)

1 onion, chopped

2 spring onions, chopped

2 garlic cloves chopped

1/2 scotch bonnet pepper, de-seeded and chopped finely

1 tsp fresh thyme leaves

2 tomatoes, de-seeded and chopped

2 x 535 g cans prepared ackees, drained, or about 24 fresh ackees, de-seeded, and picked

salt and pepper

1. If using fresh ackees, boil them in salty water for 8–10 minutes or until tender. Meanwhile, prepare the salt fish (see page 39).
2. Heat the oil in a large skillet and fry the onions, spring onions, garlic, hot pepper and thyme until the onion is transparent.
3. Add the salt fish and fry, stirring constantly, for about 3 minutes.
4. Add the tomatoes and then the ackees. Toss very lightly, trying not to break up the ackees. Sprinkle with salt and pepper to taste before serving.

Cook's tip: For a party dish you can boil some large pasta shells and stuff each one with the ackee and salt fish. Take an ovenproof casserole dish, drizzle in some olive oil and a layer of tomato sauce and sprinkle with salt and pepper and a few chopped garlic cloves. Place the stuffed shells side by side on top of the sauce and sprinkle them with grated cheese. Bake in a hot oven until the cheese melts. Serve each of the shells with a little sauce.

Aunt Sonia's Curried Shrimp

Jamaica

Aunt Sonia lives in the hills of Chapelton, in Jamaica, and is known for her many children and her sweet cooking pot. This is one of her specialities.

Preparation time: 15 minutes + 15 minutes cooking. Serves 4

2 tbsp oil

3 tbsp water

2 tbsp butter

900 g/2 lb medium to large raw prawns, shelled and de-veined

salt and pepper

For the marinade:

2 heaped tsp curry powder (Sonia prefers Trinidadian)

1 onion, chopped

1 spring onion, chopped

2 thyme sprigs

1/4 tsp brown sugar

8 garlic cloves, flattened with a heavy knife

1 tomato, de-seeded and chopped

1/2 scotch bonnet pepper, de-seeded and chopped finely

1   Mix all the marinade ingredients in a bowl, add the prawns and marinate for 15–30 minutes.

2.   Heat the oil in a large pan and brown four of the marinated garlic cloves.

3.   Add the rest of ingredients to the hot oil. Use the 3 tbsp water to rinse out the marinade bowl and gather all remnants of curry; add that to the pot. Lower the heat, cover and cook for 5 minutes.

4.   Remove the cover, stir in the butter and simmer for a further 5–10 minutes, covered. Serve immediately, with rice.

Oysters 'grow' on trees in Trinidad! These small varieties are served, often outdoors, with a dash of peppery sweet sauce.

Escoveitched Fish

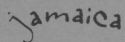
Jamaica

This pickled fish dish is quite traditional in Jamaica. You can use either fish steaks, whole fish or fillets. Any fish suitable for frying will work and even salmon is delicious when escoveitched. 'Escoveitch' mainly refers to the sauce, which is poured over the fish and absorbed after frying. It is very tangy and quite spicy when made properly. Not to be confused with 'ceviche', a raw fish salad, which is also delicious!

Escoveitch is usually eaten at room temperature and might sit out on the kitchen table for a day or two to be enjoyed as a snack by anyone who passes by. It is eaten usually at breakfast time or lunch, especially at the beach. In the evening it is a popular a dish at cocktail parties, where it will be prepared in bite-sized pieces without any bones. As a main course, it's traditionally served with bammies.

Preparation and cooking time: 30 minutes. Serves 4

1 kg/2 lb fresh snapper or tilapia fillets
1 lime
50 g/¼ cup plain flour
50 g/¼ cup cornmeal
oil, for shallow-frying
salt and pepper
125 ml/½ cup Escoveitch Pickle Sauce (see page 195), to serve

1.   Rinse the fish, drain and squeeze the juice of lime over. Season with salt and pepper.
2.   Mix the flour and cornmeal and dust the fish with it. Shake off any excess.
3.   Heat some oil in a skillet until it just starts smoking. Gently drop in the fish and fry on both sides until golden. Remove with a slotted spoon and drain on kitchen paper.
4.   Pour the escoveitch sauce over and put some of the pickled vegetable pieces on top. Serve immediately, with extra julienned vegetables.

Cook's tip: Extra julienned carrots, christophene and rings of onions heated and softened in a little vinegar for 3 minutes will make the appearance even better when serving.

Crispy Adobo Fried Fish in Coconut Oil with Okra

Jamaica

This recipe reflects the bonding of Puerto Rican and Jamaican influences. The fish is washed in lime and seasoned with a blend of adobo seasonings, allspice and hot pepper. It is dusted with a mix of cornmeal and flour (the secret to serious crispiness) before being deep-fried in coconut oil, giving it a crunchy texture outside, whilst the flesh of the fish remains juicy and succulent inside. The coconut oil adds a wonderful flavour to the spices.

As soon as the fish is finished the okra is breaded and fried in the same oil — a great way to enjoy little crunchy bits of okra.

Preparation and cooking time: 1 hour. Serves 2

For the fish:

2 red snappers, weighing about 300 g/10 oz each, scaled,
**   gutted and left whole**

1 lime

1 tbsp adobo seasoning (see page 234, or ready-made)

1 tsp ground allspice

½ scotch bonnet pepper, slivered

2 tbsp flour

2 tbsp cornmeal

coconut oil, for frying

For the okra:

6 small okras, topped tailed and cut into 1 cm/½-inch rings

1 egg, beaten

4 tbsp breadcrumbs

salt, for sprinkling

2 limes, sliced, to serve

1. First of all, wash your fish and pat dry, squeeze the juice of a lime over and inside it.

2. Make the seasoning for the fish: blend the adobo seasonings with the allspice.

3. Cut three slashes in the fish on each side and rub this mixture into the flesh. Place slivers of hot pepper in the slashes and set aside for 15 minutes.

4. Pour about 5 cm/2 inches of coconut oil into a deep-sided frying pan and put over fairly high heat. Meanwhile, mix the flour and cornmeal on a plate. Roll the fish in the flour and cornmeal mix and shake off any excess. When the oil is hot, carefully slide the fish into the pan and fry for 5–7 minutes; turn over halfway through to ensure that the fish does not burn. Carefully remove with a slotted spoon and drain on absorbent paper.

5. Keeping the oil hot, dip the okra pieces in the egg and then roll in the breadcrumbs and fry a few at a time in the hot oil until golden. Remove with a slotted spoon and place the okra on kitchen paper. When they are all done, serve immediately with the fish and a sprinkle of salt and lime slices to squeeze over.

Cook's tips: Try to find small, young okras — they are best. Do not cover either the fish or the okra or they will sweat, get soggy and lose their edge.

Countryman In the early seventies when the new road to Hellshire (just 20 minutes from Kingston, Jamaica) had been built, a few of us found our way to a small Indian fishing community on the beach and made friends with a charismatic young fisherman called 'Countryman' and his family. This was the first time I ever knew intimately the simple lifestyle of fishing folk and I came to adore my frequent visits.

We would watch him haul in the latest catch of colourful parrotfish, doctor fish and snapper. Quickly gutting a few and rinsing them in seawater. 'Mummy' would take over and deftly season and fry them in a 'wok' sitting over a fire, burning right there on the beach.

Served up with freshly fried festivals and bammies and the communal bottle of 'pickle sauce' it was a world away from any fish I had ever eaten. There, the simple food and virtually naked existence was idyllic. This was the closest I ever came to becoming a 'drop-out'.

A movie entitled and starring 'Countryman' came out in the eighties and, now, only the legend of those days lives on. Hellshire, which has expanded considerably, has become a popular spot for eating fish and swimming, especially on weekends.

Creole Fish Stew

This delicious stew is simple to make and very versatile. You can use any firm-fleshed fish and different shellfish, according to what is available at the time.

Preparation time: 25 minutes + 15 minutes cooking. Serves 4–6

2 tbsp oil

1 large onion, chopped finely

4 spring onions, trimmed and chopped finely

2 garlic cloves, chopped finely

1 hot pepper, de-seeded and chopped finely

2 x 400 g cans of tomatoes, strained with the juice reserved

1 sweet red pepper, de-seeded and cut into strips

900 g/2 lb mahi-mahi or firm fish fillets, skinned and cut
   into chunks

4 tbsp finely chopped fresh parsley

4 tbsp finely chopped fresh coriander

350ml (12 fl oz) coconut milk

450 g/1 lb cooked crab, opened, cleaned and then broken
   into pieces, or four small cooked land crabs

salt and pepper

fresh coriander sprigs, to garnish

1. Heat the oil in a medium-sized heavy-based frying-pan, add the onion, spring onions, garlic and hot pepper and fry for 5 minutes over moderate heat.

2. Add the tomatoes and sweet pepper and cook for a further 5 minutes.

3. Lay the chunks of fish in the pan and spoon over the vegetables. Sprinkle over the parsley and coriander and season to taste with salt and pepper. Pour over the coconut milk and bring to the boil.

4. Lower the heat, cover the pan and simmer for 10–15 minutes.

5. Add the cooked crab and cook for a further 5 minutes.

6. Taste, and adjust the seasoning. Transfer to a warmed serving platter and garnish with coriander.

Gundy Pasta

A totally non-traditional dish but with unmistakable Caribbean instincts. My only insistence is that you use fresh, ripe, juicy, plum tomatoes. Don't try it with canned ones as you will miss the whole point.

This dish is quick and uncomplicated if you have a jar of Gundy handy. I recommend Walkerswood Solomon Gundy for this dish unless you want to make your own. The amount of Gundy used can be varied as you like but taste it first as it has a strong flavour.

Preparation and cooking time: 20 minutes. Serves 4

450 g/1 lb penne or rigatoni pasta

6 ripe plum tomatoes, de-seeded and diced

2 garlic cloves, pressed or finely chopped

2–3 tbsp Solomon Gundy (see page 45 or Walkerswood ready-made), to taste

3 tbsp good-quality extra-virgin olive oil

2 tbsp chopped fresh parsley

1 tsp grated lime zest

salt

1.   Bring a large pot of water with 2 tsp of salt to a rolling boil. Drop in the pasta and stir. Allow to boil for 10–15 minutes or until al dente. Drain in a colander.

2.   In the meantime, combine in a large pasta bowl the tomatoes, a pinch of salt and the garlic. Add the Gundy and olive oil and stir.

3.   Add the steaming pasta to this and stir together. Add the parsley and zest and toss again. If you wish you can add a sprinkle more olive oil. Serve warm.

Court Bouillon de Poisson

Guadaloupe

Guadeloupe is famous for its seafood. A visit to the fish market in Pointe à Pitre is a dazzling experience and the fishermen will offer you all sorts of advice on how to cook their tempting catch, such as this Guadeloupian speciality, vivaneau. A 'court bouillon' here is a very simple tomato sauce, which is one of the signature dishes of the island. The light, fragrant sauce allows all the flavours of the fresh fish to emerge and this is a delicious and simple dish.

Preparation and cooking time: 25 minutes + 1 hour marinating. Serves 4

2 x 450 g/l lb vivaneau, daurades (sea bream) or red snapper, cleaned

4 garlic cloves, pressed

several thyme sprigs

1 scotch bonnet pepper, de-seeded and chopped finely

juice of 3 limes

1–2 tbsp sunflower oil

1 tablespoon roucou (annatto) oil (see page 232; optional but gives a good red colour)

2 tbsp chopped fresh chives

1 onion, chopped

3 large tomatoes, diced

salt and pepper

1. First of all, season the fish with salt and pepper, two of the garlic cloves, the sprigs of thyme, hot pepper and half the lime juice. Set aside to marinate for 1 hour.

2. Heat a tbsp of sunflower oil and add the roucou (annatto) oil, if using, or heat 2 tbsp oil if not. Add the chives and onion and sauté for just 2 minutes. Add the diced tomatoes and 2 garlic cloves cook for just 2 or 3 minutes more.

3. Add the fish, either whole or cut into pieces and then cook for 2 or 3 minutes, turning over once to seal on all sides.

4. Pour in enough water just to cover the fish, add a pinch more salt and bring to the boil. Lower the heat and simmer, covered, for 10–15 minutes, or until the fish is just cooked.

5. Just before serving, add the remaining lime juice, cook for a further 2 minutes and then serve immediately. Quite often the fish is removed, the sauce is strained and then the fish is returned to the sauce and everything warmed together before serving.

Grilled Fish Steaks with Sauce Chien

Guadaloupe

In Guadeloupe, many of the meat dishes are grilled and often served with a 'sauce chien'. This simple, traditional sauce is packed with strong flavours – Guadeloupians each have their preferred balance of ingredients so feel free to highlight any ingredients to your liking.

Preparation time: marinating 10 minutes + 1 hour infusing. Serves 4

4 marlin or dolphin fillets, or other meaty fish, seasoned with salt, pepper
 garlic and thyme
oil for brushing

For the Sauce Chien (makes 180 ml/3/4 cup/about 200 g or 5 tbsp):
1 scotch bonnet pepper, de-seeded and finely chopped
juice of 2 limes
2 tbsp finely chopped chives or spring onions
1 large onion, very finely chopped
2 garlic cloves, finely chopped
1/2 tsp fresh thyme leaves, chopped
up to 1/4 cup vegetable or olive oil
salt and freshly ground black pepper

1. First of all make the sauce chien: combine all the ingredients except the oil. This can be done in a blender, though it looks prettier if you very finely hand-cut the vegetables, etc. and then mix in oil a little at a time and allow it to sit for 1 hour.

2. Wash and dry the fish fillets and season them as described. Set aside to marinate for at least 1 hour (best for a few hours).

3. Brush a griddle with oil and also brush some on the fish. When the griddle is hot, put on the fish. Cook for about 3–4 minutes on each side, depending on the thickness. Serve with a generous spoonful of sauce chien on top.

Mixed Seafood Rice
Puerto Rico

This dish is ideal to serve at a buffet party. It's colourful and very, very tasty. The local short-grained rice in Puerto Rico is called 'rico' but any short-grained or robust 'easy-cook' rice can be used.

Preparation time 30 minutes + 50 minutes cooking. Serves 8

450 g/1 lb octopus, cleaned and cut into 5 cm/2-inch lengths

2 tbsp olive oil

1 large onion, diced

1 sweet red pepper, de-seeded and cut into squares

125 g/4 oz Spanish chorizo sausage, cubed roughly

2 garlic cloves, pressed

1 heaped tsp paprika

½ tsp cayenne pepper

1 tsp ground turmeric or 1 tsp annatto oil (see page 232)

225 g/8 oz firm, ripe tomatoes, skinned and roughly diced

1 litre/1¾ pints boiling water

350 g/12 oz short-grained (paella) or easy-cook rice

450 g/1 lb raw or cooked prawns

450 g/1 lb fresh mussels or small clams, scrubbed
    and de-bearded

175 g/6 oz fresh or frozen peas

salt and pepper

1 lime, cut into wedges, to garnish

For the seasoning:

juice of 1 lime

2 garlic cloves, crushed

2 spring onions, chopped roughly

1 tsp dried thyme

½ tsp de-seeded and finely chopped scotch bonnet pepper

1. First of all blend the ingredients for the seasoning together in a blender or mortar and pestle and season the octopus. Set aside.

2. Heat the oil in a heavy-based frying pan over medium heat. Add the onion, sweet pepper and chorizo and cook over medium heat for about 5 minutes. Add the garlic, paprika, cayenne pepper, turmeric or annatto oil and cook for a further minute.

3. Add the octopus and the marinade, the tomatoes and the water, bring to the boil, reduce the heat and simmer for 10 minutes.

4. Stir in the rice and bring everything back to the boil and then lower the heat and simmer, uncovered for 10 minutes.

5. Add the prawns and mussels or clams to the pan as well as the peas and cover for 20–30 minutes, or until the rice is cooked and the liquid absorbed. (Add more hot liquid only if necessary.) To test if the rice is done, taste some rice from the side of the pan which will take the longest to cook. When cooked, toss everything and serve immediately.

Cook's tip: If you are unable to find any mussels or clams or if you prefer, use lobster or crabs instead, chopped up.

poultry

SAUCY SAUTÉS & SIZZLING BROILERS

Having been chased by a rooster as a child I never had much use for them as pets, but I had a great deal of love for Holly and Ivy, a duck and a goose who, unknown to us, were being fattened up, in our own backyard, for the holidays. Christmas dinner that year was grief and my Mum and Dad, who had grown up comfortably with the rituals of farm life, could not fathom what had gotten into their two hysterical daughters, when faced with such a delicious feast. When asked what was wrong I wailed, 'I – don't – eat – my – friends!'.

It is one of those paradoxes that we somehow learn to deal with and I feel sure that some of the things we refuse to eat now could be at the top of our list if we had been introduced to their delights as a child. I now like to eat goose and duck and, like most of my compatriots, eat a lot of chicken. We tend to prepare it mostly on the bone and the brown meat is every bit as well liked as the breast. To be honest I think most of us islanders prefer the more succulent thigh and leg parts.

We eat chicken cooked in every conceivable way throughout the islands. For many it is the highpoint of the week when prepared for Sunday dinner. I had delicious free-range 'ragout de coq' in Guadeloupe: it was quite meaty, and not at all dry. Free-range is the best-tasting poultry and somewhat more humane if you care about that sort of thing. In Jamaica 'jerk chicken' has grown in popularity. It is inexpensive and readily available.

Duck is less common unless you have a farm, but it is quite popular with the East Indian community in Trinidad. Curried duck is the main item at a 'river lime', which is a family picnic held by the river. This type of cooking is called 'three-stone cooking', wherein a large pot, a 'dutchie' or kerosene oil pan is balanced on stones over an outdoor fire.

Boiled Chicken with Sizzling Escallion Oil

Jamaican-Chinese

This dish still remains one of my favourites. I learned to make it years ago in the kitchen of one of my Chinese-Jamaican friends. It is very simple yet satisfying and fun to eat with chopsticks and dipping bowls. It's a casual and messy process even if you are deft with chopsticks, so be prepared to wipe your chin.

Preparation time: 10 minutes + 45 minutes cooking time. Serves 6

3 tbsp oyster sauce (optional)

1–2 tsp salt

1 chicken, washed and all cavities cleaned

For dipping:

60 ml/½ cup peanut or other vegetable oil

4 tbsp finely chopped spring onion, green and white parts

60 ml/¼ cup soya sauce

1 scotch bonnet pepper, sliced (optional)

1. Fill a large pot about half full of water. Bring to the boil. Drop in the oyster sauce, salt and the whole chicken.
2. Skim the water occasionally as the chicken boils. It will take about 45 minutes to be thoroughly cooked.
3. Remove the chicken from the water and place on a platter. Depending on how informal the setting you can either take it to the table and let everyone pick their pieces or do it in the kitchen. Remove the skin and then pull all the flesh off in strips. Put the chicken meat in a bowl. (The cooking liquid can be reserved for use as stock; skim off the fat when cold.)
4. In a small saucepan, heat the oil. Place the spring onions in a heat-resistant bowl and, when the oil is really hot, pour it over them. The oil will sizzle.
5. Meanwhile, place small bowls of soya sauce around, some with slices of hot pepper in, some plain.
6. Serve with small bowls of rice if you wish, but really it's just a casual snack wherein the chicken is dipped first in the soya sauce then in the oil. Eat and repeat.

Chicken Pelau

Trinidad

This is to Trinidad what curried goat is to Jamaica – a serious tradition. This version is from Pat Tracey's mother. She does not use precise measurements so we have done our best...

Preparation time: 1 hour marinating + 30 minutes + 30 minutes cooking. Serves 6

1 medium chicken, cut into pieces
1 tbsp cane vinegar or distilled malt (white)
    vinegar
2 onions, chopped
3 thyme sprigs
3 garlic cloves, pressed
salt and pepper
2–3 tbsp vegetable oil

2 tbsp brown sugar
1 sweet pepper, chopped
1/2 cup diced pumpkin (optional)
2 cups rice, parboiled
110 ml/1/2 cup coconut milk
up to 1 litre/41/2 cups water
whole hot pepper

1.   Wash the chicken in salt water and pat dry. Season with vinegar, onion, thyme, garlic, salt and pepper. Cover and refrigerate overnight.

2.   Heat the oil in a large flameproof casserole. Add the sugar and allow to caramelise. It will bubble and froth but don't let it burn.

3.   Reserve the seasoning from chicken and add the pieces a few at at time to the casserole. Turn them until the chicken is all browned.

4.   Add the drained and reserved seasonings and sweet pepper and pumpkin and stir together. Simmer for 5 minutes and then add the rice, making sure everything is well mixed together. Add a pinch of salt.

5.   Add the coconut milk and the water. Stir (make sure the rice is covered by about 2.5cm/1 inch of liquid) and then drop in whole pepper and bring to the boil. Do not allow the pepper to burst or the pelau will be very hot.

6.   Immediately reduce the heat, cover and steam on a low heat for about 35 minutes, until the rice is cooked. Do not open or stir while cooking, but fluff up just before serving.

Coq au Rhum

This method of cooking the chicken is quite similar to a fricassee with the choice of spices and tomatoes, but it achieves a mysterious depth with the addition of the dark rum and cream. Even though a fair amount of rum is used, the flavour is a lot subtler than you might expect. A bit of a twist on a traditional dish.

Preparation time: 10 minutes + 2 hours marinating + 30 minutes cooking. Serves 4

1 chicken, jointed, skin left on (unless you insist)

juice of 1 lime

1 tbsp oil

1 tbsp cooking oil (use more if you skin the
    chicken)

180 ml/¾ cup dark rum

1 tsp allspice berries or (½ tsp ground allspice)

2 bay leaves

250 g/9 oz tomatoes, skinned and de-seeded

1 potato, peeled and cubed

½ cup water

1 cup sliced mushrooms

125 ml/½ cup cream (this is delicious, but
    optional)

salt and pepper

For the seasoning:

1 onion

½ or 1 scotch bonnet pepper, de-seeded

4 spring onions

3 garlic cloves

1. Wash the chicken in salty water and then pat dry and squeeze the lime juice over.
2. Finely chop all the seasoning ingredients together and rub all over chicken. Cover and refrigerate for at least 2 hours or up to a day.
3. Heat the oil in a large pot. Brush most of the seasoning off chicken and reserve. Brown the pieces of chicken (three pieces a time); then remove and keep aside.
4. Add the reserved seasoning to the pot and allow the onions to become transparent.
5. De-glaze the pot with about ¼ cup of the rum, scraping all the sticky bits of browned chicken from the bottom, and then add the chicken pieces, allspice, bay leaves, tomatoes, potato and water. Bring to a boil, then turn down heat, cover and simmer for about 25 minutes until thoroughly cooked. (The potato will blend in to thicken the sauce.) Add a little more water if you find it is necessary.
6. Remove the chicken. If you prefer a smooth sauce it can be strained at this stage.
7. Add the mushrooms and the rest of the rum and simmer for 5 more minutes until the alcohol evaporates. Remove the chicken. Skim off any excess oil. (If you prefer a smooth sauce it can be strained at this stage.)
8. Then stir in the cream, if using, check the seasoning and pour the sauce over the warm chicken to serve.

Swanky Chicken Rundown

'Oiled down', 'rundown', these are simply descriptions of cooking with coconut milk and seasonings until the liquid reduces and forms a thick gravy. You'll get a superior flavour if you use fresh coconut milk, but making it will take a little time (see Cook's Notes). If you prefer to use prepared, powdered coconut is a good substitute for this dish as you can make it a bit thicker than canned coconut milk and this way, save on cooking time. I have chosen to use boneless breast as it makes for a quick and attractive finish.

Because of the white wine and cream this is quite a rich dish but really delicious and easy to make. It is so foolproof, this one will make you look like you know what you are doing in the kitchen, even if you don't.

Preparation time: 1 hour marinating 60 minutes + 40 minutes. Serves 4–6

4 boneless, skinless chicken breasts, cut into 3 cm/1½ inch cubes	6 allspice berries (or ¼ tsp ground allspice powder)
1 tsp fresh thyme, leaves chopped	1 spring onion, finely chopped
2 garlic cloves, minced	2 tbsp cooking oil
½ tsp salt and a dash of white pepper	110 ml/¼ cup dry white wine
180 ml/¾ cup coconut milk powder, mixed as instructed	110 ml/¼ cup double cream
½ scotch bonnet pepper, de-seeded and minced	1 tbsp chopped fresh coriander, to garnish

1. Wash and cut up the chicken, season with the thyme, garlic, onion and salt and pepper, cover and refrigerate for an hour if you can.
2. Mix the coconut powder and water to make milk. Add the scotch bonnet, allspice and spring onion and cook for 10–15 minutes (don't cover). Allow the coconut milk to simmer and reduce, but turn down the heat and add a little more powder if it is too thin.
3. In a large flameproof casserole or skillet, heat the oil and then add the chicken. Seal all the pieces of chicken by stirring them in the hot oil for about 8 minutes. (Don't allow the chicken to get too brown or it will discolour your gravy.)
4. De-glaze the pot with the white wine and stir for 2 minutes, until most of it is absorbed.
5. Add the thickened coconut milk and cream, stir and simmer for another minute. Remove from the heat and sprinkle with coriander to garnish. Serve with Pumpkin Rice (see page 169) and salad. Light the candles...

Cook's tip: Use 'coconut rundown sauce' as a substitute for the coconut milk, but add it at the end with the cream as it has already been spiced and reduced.

Five-spice Roast Chicken

The longer the chicken is marinated, the more intense the flavour will be. This recipe is also delicious if you 'spatchcock' the chicken to be cooked on the barbecue. For a Sunday roast, I recommend surrounding the whole chicken with roasted potatoes and extra garlic in the roasting pan.

Preparation time: marinating + 20 minutes+ 1½ hours cooking. Serves 4

1.6 kg/3 lb 5 oz chicken

juice of 1 lime

2 tbsp light soya sauce

2 tbsp honey

4 cinnamon sticks

6 star anise

6 cardamom pods

6 cloves

6 allspice berries

2 garlic cloves, chopped

6 garlic cloves, peeled but left whole

1 hot pepper, cut in two

1. Wash the chicken and pat dry with kitchen paper. Rub the lime juice over the chicken and set aside for 10 minutes.

2. Mix the soya sauce and honey together in a small bowl. Crush half the cinnamon sticks and star anise, all of the cardamom pods, cloves and allspice berries and two of the garlic cloves together with a mortar and pestle. Rub into the chicken. Cover with foil and place in the fridge to marinate overnight.

3. Preheat the oven to 170°C/325°F/Gas Mark 3.

4. Remove the chicken from the fridge, transfer to a roasting tin and add the remaining garlic cloves, cinnamon sticks and star anise. Tuck the hot pepper into the main cavity (remove before serving). Bake in the oven for 1–1½ hours, or until the chicken is cooked through, basting from time to time. Serve immediately.

Cook's tip: To spatchcock a chicken, using a sharp knife or poultry shears, cut through the backbone of the chicken and open out the bird, flattening it firmly with the palm of your hand. To keep it flat, you can use metal skewers or long wooden satay sticks, pushed diagonally through the bird. This method hastens cooking time.

Spiced Duck with Tamarind Sauce

Duck is not commercially popular in the Caribbean but many people with space raise a few for themselves. In Trinidad, curried duck is a popular feature at a 'river lime' (riverside picnic).

This dish is quite easy to prepare and you can cook to the level of doneness you prefer.

Preparation and cooking time: 50 minutes. Serves 4

For the duck breasts:

4 duck breasts

2 garlic cloves, crushed

about ½ tsp salt

1 tsp five-spice powder

For the tamarind sauce:

80 ml/⅓ cup Red Pepper Jelly (see page 197)

4 tbsp hot water

2 tbsp cane vinegar or distilled (white) malt vinegar

1 tbsp tamarind paste

2 garlic cloves, finely chopped

1 tsp sugar

1 tbsp chopped fresh coriander

1. Preheat the oven to 200°C/400°F/Gas Mark 6.
2. Score the duck breasts into a diamond pattern with a sharp knife, just cutting through the skin and fat but not the flesh. Then rub them all over the with garlic, salt to taste and the five-spice powder. Set aside for 30 minutes while you make the sauce.
3. Put all the ingredients for the sauce together in a saucepan. Cook over moderate heat until the pepper jelly has melted, stirring constantly. Reduce the heat to lower and simmer for 10 minutes, or longer if necessary to thicken slightly, stirring constantly. Remove from the heat.
4. Place the duck breasts, skin-sides down, in a non-stick frying pan over low heat. Once the fat begins to melt, increase the heat to medium-high and fry for about 5 minutes. Turn them over and continue to fry until the meat is cooked to your liking. After 5–6 minutes the duck will be pink inside. If you prefer it more well cooked, continue cooking in a moderate oven for a further 5 minutes.
5. Reheat the sauce and serve immediately with the duck, which you should serve sliced.

Ginger & Garlic Chicken with a Sweet Barbecue Sauce

The secret to all grilled or roasted chicken is to season or marinate it well before cooking. This dish can be either cooked in the oven or on a barbecue.

Preparation time: 15 minutes + marinating overnight + 1½ hours cooking. Serves 4–6

1.5 kg/3½ lb chicken, spatchcocked (see Cook's tip, page 110)

4 garlic cloves, crushed

5 cm/2 in piece of fresh root ginger, peeled and grated

For the barbecue sauce:

310 ml/1¼ cups tomato ketchup

2 tbsp honey

2 tsp molasses (optional)

2 tbsp Pickapeppa sauce or Worcestershire sauce

1 tsp hot mustard

juice of 1 lime

about 1 tsp hot pepper sauce

1 tsp salt

freshly ground black pepper

60ml/¼ cup water

watercress, to garnish

1. Make the sauce: put the tomato ketchup, honey, molasses, sauce, mustard, lime juice, pepper sauce, salt, pepper and water into a saucepan and bring to the boil, stirring constantly. Cook for a couple of minutes, until all the ingredients are thoroughly combined. Remove from the heat and set aside to cool.

2. Wash and dry the chicken and then, using a sharp knife, score the chicken across the breast legs, thighs, making quite deep cuts to allow the seasoning to penetrate into the flesh.

3. Mix the garlic and grated ginger together to make a paste and spread it over the chicken, pressing it into the cuts in the skin. Spoon over a quarter of the barbecue sauce and rub it well into the skin. Cover and leave to marinate in the fridge overnight.

4. Preheat the oven to 180°C/350°F/Gas Mark 4. Place the chicken in a roasting tin. Spoon the remaining barbecue sauce over the chicken and place in the oven to roast for 1¼–1½ hours, basting constantly.

5. Transfer to a serving platter, garnish with some watercress and serve immediately.

Dressed-up Curried Chicken

Some people add coconut milk to curries and some don't. It adds richness to the flavour but leave it out if you prefer. Jamaican curry does differ from, say, Trinidadian and the truth is that curries can vary greatly depending on the different blends of spices. It's nice if you can find one made in the region you are visiting but this too is not critical. Serve with a good fruit chutney and rice.

Preparation and cooking time: 3 hours marinating + 30 minutes. Serves 6

6 boneless, skinless chicken breasts, washed

salt and pepper

oil, for browning

3 cardamom pods

2 tomatoes, skinned, de-seeded and chopped

60 ml/½ cup coconut milk

about 60 ml/½ cup water

25 g/1 oz raisins

For the seasoning:

2 spring onions

2 thyme sprigs

½ scotch bonnet pepper, sliced

1 onion, chopped

2 garlic cloves, pressed

4 tsp West Indian curry powder or paste

To garnish:

25 g/1 oz sliced almonds, toasted

chopped fresh parsley

2 tbsp freshly grated coconut (optional)

1. Wash the chicken, pat dry and cut into 5 cm/2-inch chunks. Rub in the seasonings. (Don't handle the scotch bonnet if you are not accustomed to it; just use a spoon and mix it in last.) Leave to marinate for 3 hours if possible.

2. Heat the oil in a large skillet. Brush off the seasoning from the chicken pieces and reserve. Brown the chicken pieces for 5–6 minutes and then add the reserved seasonings, cardamom pods and tomatoes. Cook gently for 1 minute.

3. Add the coconut milk and stir in, scraping in the browned bits in the pan. Allow the chicken to come to a simmer and then add some of the water and stir again (you can always add more water if it begins to stick). After 4 minutes, check the seasoning, add the raisins and cook for 1 more minute before removing from heat. Sprinkle with toasted almonds, fresh parsley and freshly grated coconut, if using, before serving.

jerk

TRADITIONAL, CONTEMPORARY & SERIOUSLY HOT

Something about Jerk To find jerk, we should go to the land of 'Look Behind' (historical Maroon country in Jamaica, where the British army feared to tread).

Jerk is the Jamaican way of preparing highly seasoned meat, slowly cooked over a fire-pit of pimento wood, whereupon the food remains tender and delights the consumer with its hot, succulent and aromatic blend of earthy Caribbean deliciousness!

One might hear differing tales of how jerk came about, but there is little question that it is a Jamaican tradition. The most popular notion is that the Maroons perfected it, that they probably came with the basics from their African homeland and that they may have acquired a trick or two from the original Jamaicans, the Tainos (the Tainos, Caribs and Arawaks were the indigenous Caribbean peoples who taught the buccaneers how to barbecue). The Maroons were African slaves who were freed and left behind in Jamaica by the Spanish and they defied capture by the British when they took over the island. Being fierce resisters, they survived mainly in the rugged terrain of the Cockpit Country – the most inhospitable part of the island, which is riddled with limestone caves – and across the mountainous spine of the island as far east as the Blue Mountains. They endured through their bravery and skill and hunted and cooked the wild pigs that had been left behind by the Spanish. This was probably the birth of jerk as we know it today.

They hunted with packs of highly trained dogs, which they used efficiently. This meat needed to be cooked and stored so they could move around for a few days at a time and avoid the British. The determined British soldiers rode 'two on a horse': facing both ways in their effort to avoid ambush by the Maroons, so smoke from cooking fires would have been kept to a minimum. The spicy seasoning was probably the secret of the Maroons' method of curing – not the more common salting or smoking of the meat.

The Maroons eventually attained a treaty with the British and gained freedom to live in their own lands. They kept to themselves for many years and, after emancipation, they would go to rural markets and carry with them portions of 'jerk pork', which were sold from specially constructed pouches called *intetehs*, woven from palm leaves. The jerk pork was always well received but for a long time its preparation remained a secret. It was only about 50 years ago that a version of the jerk recipe came out of the hills and started to be prepared openly. This happened first in Portland, on the lowlands below Moore Town, one of the few Maroon settlements (others being Accompong, and Maroon Town, Westmoreland), which is where my grandmother was born. Visitors from all over the world have come to document the unique story of the Maroons, who have a fascinating history.

The name jerk, which is always difficult to explain, especially given the modern associations and connotations, was probably derived from an English word 'jirk', a corruption of the Spanish *charqui* – the word for dried meat. I suspect that, as with so many other traditions, there will always be room for other interpretations.

Modern Jerk I never heard of jerk until I was a teenager, when we went to Portland (on the north coast of Jamaica) for swimming, surfing, water-skiing and fun in the sun. Boston Bay, one of the beaches we haunted, had become the place for it and jerk was certainly moreish. Checking back with friends, some were aware of it from the 60s but it did not turn up on the menu or on the mainstream dinner table in Jamaica until 20 years later. The wide popularity of jerk is relatively new. After Boston Bay (still the most famous), jerk pits emerged in Montego Bay and in Kingston, but it was still regarded mainly as street food.

Traditionally only pork was jerked but at the time jerk was becoming all the rage (in the 70s), Rastafarianism was becoming more influential, with the advent of Bob Marley, and vegetarianism was becoming quite trendy. Rastafarians might tolerate jerk fish and fowl but pork and pork-eaters are way off limits. Quite soon, jerk chicken overtook pork in popularity. In the 70s there were efforts to research and bottle the essential jerk seasoning. Walkerswood Caribbean Foods (then known as Cottage Industries) was the first Jamaican company to bottle jerk seasoning commercially and the first to export it (see The Walkerswood Story, page 124). Once the essence of jerk was being bottled commercially (now by several companies) it was more available and cooks started experimenting with fish, lamb and just about anything you can safely imagine. Jerk seasoning moved into the urban kitchen and its reputation grew like wildfire! As a result of this surge in popularity, 'jerk centres' started appearing in towns and villages and 'jerk pans' were set up on many street corners. (A jerk pan is an oil drum cut in half, set horizontally on legs with a wire rack, a hinged top with a handle and a hole cut in the bottom half to let air in. It's a simple but effective barbecue grill.) Some vendors sell 'pan-chicken' (barbecued), while others sell jerk chicken or pork.

Since the 80s, exports of jerk seasoning have been skyrocketing. Jamaican companies have since obliged by making it more available to the mainstream markets in Europe and North America and as far as South Africa and Japan. I can safely say that jerk is probably now the most widely recognised flavour from the Caribbean.

We will never quite replicate that original Maroon jerk, which is really a method of cooking, but we are always looking for quicker ways to achieve good results and if handled properly the seasoning will give you a delicious jerk at home. Barbecued, oven and even stove-top versions can be really tasty. Jerk seasoning is not so mysterious and you'll probably find that most of the ingredients are already in your kitchen but, if you can't be bothered to make it from scratch, there are some excellent commercial ones on the market.

A Few Pointers on Making Traditional Jerk As so few people will actually build a jerk pit in their yard, or find pimento wood to put over their fire, I will assume that the best we can do is a barbecue grill with hot coals and a cover. It really will make a good jerk. It's good enough for me!

Use a large cut of meat. By that I mean half chickens, a pork shoulder, a boneless leg of lamb or something similar. You will get better flavour and texture if you use something which won't cook too fast. Since jerk is traditionally a hot and spicy dish, I am a bit opposed to those who water it down. In trying to appeal to everyone, they boast that they eat or sell jerk when what they actually have is just a spicy barbecue.

I don't think you have to kill yourself with the pepper either, though, and the best way to avoid this is to marinate your food properly. This way all the flavours have a chance to permeate the meat subtly. Try your best to marinate overnight. This is one of the secrets to good jerk. Give it at least a few hours or you won't get the best results.

Another key point is to go easy on quantity. You should not use too much seasoning for your rub or you will totally overpower what you are cooking. You over-doers give jerk a bad name.

Build a slow fire. The coals should be burning white. Brush the grill with oil to prevent sticking. You should not be seeing any flames when the meat goes on.

Cook your pork, lamb and chicken in its skin; this will add considerably to the flavour. You can throw it away after, if you must.

Cover the meat for least a part of the cooking time so a bit of steaming takes place and the meat doesn't dry out.

Cook it long and slowly and turn once or twice. Again, jerk is not barbecue; you are not looking for a charred, blackened finish and the meat should not burn.

When it's done, the meat should be falling off the bone: there is no 'rare' or 'medium' in traditional jerk.

I have seen people adding fresh jerk seasoning to their cooked jerk meat, but this should not be necessary (some of us just can't help ourselves).

Non-traditional Versions of Jerk For this section you'll need to forget everything I said about traditional jerk in the section above, grab your jar of jerk seasoning and see what else you can do. I have now heard of everything from jerk sushi to jerk alligator. What next? Well that is up to all of us, because it seems that with a developing cuisine the things that people like and cook over and over are the recipes that get on the menu and stick.

If you like the flavour of jerk you will do as many Jamaicans do and start using it as an all-purpose seasoning. The highnotes are the allspice, the peppers, spring onion and cinnamon. These are all strong flavours so you need to use jerk sparingly and think about what other resilient foods you will need to balance it. Grab your grill pan, oven or casserole dish if necessary. I only draw a line here at the microwave.

I think jerk is fabulous in combination with meat, chicken or seafood with tomatoes and pasta (see Jerk Chicken Pasta, page 140). There's nothing wrong with a dash of wine to de-glaze your grill pan, as the same recipe shows, and jerk also takes cream well, which serves to tone it down.

Since hot and sweet is so nice, contrast between filling and the sweet potato topping in the Picadillo Pie recipe (page 153) will be a treat and Honey Jerk Seasoning (page 127) is the 'boom'. I sprinkle dried jerk seasoning on my cheese omelettes because it tastes great (page 141) and now you can even buy jerk cheese and sausages. If you love jerk you will find many ways of using it.

The Walkerswood Story In the 80s I started to visit a sleepy little village some 40 miles away from Kingston (the bustling capital of Jamaica), and just 9 miles from Ocho Rios, the popular tourist resort. My sister Nancy had moved into the rural paradise of Walkerswood, employing the skilled hands of a few villagers to help produce her art and craft designs. Home was what used to be the old schoolhouse on the Bromley property. A stunningly beautiful location, central to the village, surrounded by hills and pastureland .

During frequent visits, it soon became apparent to me that though small, this was an extraordinary community. Here, the people had pulled together and, with the benefit of some vision and leadership, they had formed a Community Council. The council's employment committee started a sustainable development based on jerk seasoning. Not only was it worker-owned (it still is), but its goal was to provide jobs for those who wanted to remain in the countryside. Cottage Industries was the original name of the company (formed in 1978) which later became Walkerswood Caribbean Foods.

'Cottage' as it was fondly known had developed a delicious recipe for jerk seasoning based on research done in Portland, the home of the Maroons. It became the first company in Jamaica to bottle the seasoning and the first to export it. This was serious pioneering work and required the support of local farmers and a whole range of initiatives.

When the history is written, much credit for the introduction of Jamaican jerk food overseas will have to be given to WCF. Seen as an exemplary Jamaican company, this unique business did not employ experts in the food industry – it has attempted to create them. Walkerswood Caribbean Foods bottles traditional Caribbean sauces, spices and condiments and the company has ventured further into farming and restaurants as a means to continue the development. Nevertheless, jerk seasoning is still the lifeblood as both the business and the community continue to grow.

Thus started a fascinating journey for me, which has led to the writing of this book.

Jerk Seasoning

Jamaica

If you check out various brands and recipes for jerk seasoning and marinades, you will find a variety of ingredients in them that certainly did not exist when the Marooons were developing the method. I have seen soya sauce, rum, mustard and ketchup and it seems that everyone has their 'secret ingredient'. The following ingredients are the most essential and should be included: allspice berries, hot pepper (scotch bonnet and birdpepper), spring onion, ginger, cinnamon, thyme and black pepper.

The recipe below is simple and based on research and repeated success. The amount of jerk to use can vary quite a bit and most people learn to use it through trial. You can make your seasoning mild or create a batch of 'lip remover'. Even the peppers vary in strength. Always use less rather than more until you get the hang of it.

Preparation time: 10 minutes. Makes: about 180 ml/²/3 cup

6 spring onions

1–3 scotch bonnet peppers (use 1 pepper if you don't want it
  seriously hot!)

2 tsp allspice berries or 1 tsp ground allspice

1 tbsp chopped fresh thyme or ¹/2 tbsp dried thyme

2 tsp ground cinnamon

1 tsp grated nutmcg

1 tsp brown sugar

1¹/2 tsp salt

1 tsp freshly ground black pepper

¹/4 cup cane vinegar or distilled (white) malt vinegar

1 tbsp oil

1. The traditional method is to crudely mash all the ingredients up with a mortar and pestle and use to marinate the meat, discarding any large bits of spring onion, etc, before cooking. To make it easier, you can use a blender to reduce all the ingredients to a thick paste.

Honey Jerk Seasoning

This recipe works particularly well with pork, lamb or chicken.
Makes 60 ml/¹/4 cup (enough to marinate 900 g/2 lb meat)

¹/4 cup Jerk Seasoning (see above)

2 tsp finely minced fresh root ginger

2 tbsp honey

1. Mix all the ingredients together in a small bowl.

Lime and Garlic Jerk Mayonnaise

Certainly home-made mayonnaise would be ideal for this but it's so much easier to use a good commercial one – I wouldn't think twice. It's ideal for perking up sandwiches, burgers, fish, coleslaw and egg, chicken or tuna salads.

Preparation time: 5 minutes. Makes 225 ml/1 cup

225 ml/1 cup mayonnaise
1 tsp Jerk Seasoning (see page 127, or Walkerswood ready-made)
1 garlic clove, pressed or very finely chopped
juice of ½ lime

1. Mix everything together and spread it on!

Garlic Jerk Butter with Lime

Great for topping fish, steak, chicken, rice or vegetables or smeared on slices of your favourite bread and toasted. You'll probably like keeping a little bowlful on hand in the fridge for a quick taste solution.

Preparation time: 10 minutes + 30 minutes chilling. Makes about 60 ml/¼ cup

50 g/2 oz butter, softened
1 garlic clove, pressed
½ tsp Jerk Seasoning (see page 127, or Walkerswood ready-made)
1 tbsp lime juice
½ tbsp finely chopped fresh coriander or parsley
1 tsp grated lime zest

1. Put all the ingredients in a bowl and mix with a hand blender or whisk. Chill until ready to use.

Jerk Barbecue Sauce

This sauce is not raging hot and yet has those wonderful jerk spices lingering in the background. It's quite family friendly.

Preparation time: 10 minutes. Makes about 300 ml/½ pint (enough to marinate 2.25 kg/5 lb meat)

300 ml/1½ pints tomato ketchup

2 tbsp honey

2 tsp molasses or tamarind paste (optional)

2 tbsp Pickapeppa sauce or Worcestershire sauce

1 tsp hot mustard

juice of 1 lime

1 tbsp Jerk Seasoning (see page 127, or Walkerswood ready-made)

1 tsp salt

1.　Simply mix all the ingredients together.

Jerk Mustard

This makes a delectable topping for burgers or steak.

Preparation time: 5 minutes. Serves 6

3 tbsp Dijon mustard

1 tsp lime juice

1½ tsp Jerk Seasoning (see page 127, or Walkerswood ready-made)

1.　Put the mustard in a small bowl, add the lime juice and jerk seasoning and mix together. Put on your hot burger or steak just before serving.

Grilled Jerk Chicken

Jerk Chicken is a hot and spicy traditional Jamaican dish. You can always adjust the amount of seasoning used, to your taste, but this recipe is the typical spicy version.

Preparation time: 1 hour or overnight marinating + 40 minutes cooking. Serves 4–6

1 fresh lime (or lemon)
1.5 kg/1 lb 5 oz chicken, jointed (skin on)
2 tablespoons Jerk Seasoning (see page 127, or Walkerswood ready-made)
oil, for brushing

1. Squeeze the lime or lemon juice into a bowl of water and rinse the chicken. Pat dry. Rub the jerk seasoning all over the chicken and leave to marinate for a minimum of 1 hour or overnight.
2. Light the barbecue and get it so the coals are covered with a layer of white ash. Brush the chicken and the grill with oil. Cook the chicken over a medium heat for about 20 minutes. Then cover the barbecue and cook for a further 20 minutes or until done.

Jerk Pork

Since wild pigs were the earliest source of jerked meat, pork is still regarded as the most traditional jerk dish. Getting a large piece of pork jerked to perfection will take a proper barbecue set-up, as it is essential to keep the meat juicy and succulent while slow-cooking it thoroughly and getting the flavours through. This is where the smoking allspice wood really plays its part and there is little one can do to substitute for it.

However, for home-style jerk pork which is almost as delicious, use pork loin or chops and leave the fat on while cooking. Rub with the desired amount of jerk seasoning and allow to marinate overnight of for a few hours before grilling or roasting. The centre of the pork should read 170°C on a meat thermometer to be properly done.

Pork is particularly tasty basted with Honey Jerk Seasoning (see page 127).

Cook's tips: Next time you roast a turkey, consider massaging jerk seasoning inside and out and marinating overnight – then proceed to cook as usual.

Guava glaze (see page 190) adds a lick for those who like it both hot and sweet!

Jerked Lamb with Guava Sauce

With this dish the heat from the jerk seasoning remains on the outside of the roast and most people will consider it spicy but not too hot. Allow the full time for marinating so that you get the best results.

Preparation time: 15 minutes + marinating overnight + about 1 hour cooking. Serves 8–10

2.5 kg/5 lb boned leg of lamb or lamb cutlets
3 tbsp (less if using cutlets) Jerk Seasoning (see page 127 or Walkerswood)
about 2 tsp salt
2 garlic cloves, crushed
Guava Dipping Sauce (see page 190), warmed, to serve

1. Rub the jerk seasoning and salt to taste into the lamb thoroughly. Cover and marinate in the fridge overnight.
2. Preheat the oven to 180C/350F/Gas Mark 4. Rub the crushed garlic into the inside of the lamb leg and then roll it up and tie in three places to secure. Roast for 45 minutes (medium rare) or about 15 minutes more for well done lamb. If using cutlets, spread the crushed garlic over them and grill for 8–10 minutes on both sides.
3. Allow the lamb to rest for 10 minutes before carving. Slice the lamb and serve with the warm sauce.

Cook's tip: Naturally you can bake or grill jerked lamb, or chops or, basically, any other cut, adjusting the amount of seasoning and the cooking times accordingly (see Jerk Kebabs, page 57).

Jerk Fish with Lime & Garlic Jerk Butter

This dish could hardly be simpler. When marinating fish and seafood with jerk seasoning, it does not take as long as with meat, but you should still try and give it some time. You can jerk just about any kind of fish but use your discretion with those with very delicate flesh. This meal is great with creamy mashed cassava, yam or potatoes and a side dish of greens.
Preparation and cooking time: up to 2 hours marinating + 10 minutes. Serves 4

4 fish steaks (use any firm fish)
juice of 1 lime
1–2 tsp Jerk Seasoning (see page 127, or Walkerswood ready-made)
butter or oil for greasing
To serve:
1 lime, quartered
Garlic Jerk Butter with Lime (see page 128)

1. Wash the fish with the lime juice and rub in the jerk seasoning. Wrap in cling film and refrigerate for ½ hour or up to 2 hours. Light the barbecue or preheat the grill.
2. Place the fish on an oiled grill rack or on the barbecue, brush with oil and grill on either side until just done. This will take about 3–5 minutes on each side, depending on the thickness of the fish.
3. Garnish with lime pieces and serve with the lime and garlic jerk butter.

Cook's tip: Instead of grilling, you can wrap the fish in greased foil and bake it at 180°C/350°F/ Gas Mark 4 for about 15 minutes. It will steam in its own juices.

Jerk Mixed Grill

Here are a few ingredients which are easy to skewer. Brush them with Jerk Barbecue Sauce (see page 129) or Honey Jerk Seasoning (see page 127) and you'll end up with a foolproof platter of delicious food.

Preparation and cooking time: 1 hour marinating + 25 minutes. Serves 4

Honey jerk meat:

450 g/1 lb boneless chicken, or boneless, tender lamb, pork, or beef, cut into 5-cm/2-inch cubes

1/2 tsp salt

60 ml/1/4 cup Honey Jerk Seasoning (see page 127)

Gingery barbecued fish and seafood:

450 g/1 lb fresh snapper, mahi-mahi, king fish or other firm fish steaks, cut into 5-cm/2-inch pieces, (prawns and scallops will also work)

125 ml/1/4 cup Jerk Barbecue Sauce (see page 129)

2 tsp finely grated fresh root ginger

1. Rub the chicken or meat cubes with the salt and then place in a bowl, with the honey jerk sauce. Mix well and leave to marinate for at least 1 hour before threading on to skewers.

2. Season the fish or seafood with salt. Then mix together the jerk barbecue sauce and ginger in a bowl. Add the fish and marinate for 20 minutes before threading on to skewers.

3. Get the barbecue hot, so that the coals are covered with a layer of white ash. Then start with pork skewers, if you have them, because they will take the longest. Allow 5–7 minutes per side on medium-hot heat. Cook chicken and beef for 4–5 minutes on each side and fish and shellfish for 3–5 minutes per side. Baste and turn as you go along, until cooked.

Cook's tip: Remember to oil the grill rack so your pieces of meat won't stick; and soak wooden skewers in water for an hour beforehand so they won't burn.

Supreme Jerk Burger

This burger recipe is definitely a step up from the usual.
Preparation time: 30 minutes chilling + 15 minutes cooking + 10 minutes. Serves 6

2 tbsp butter or enough for sautéing

1 onion, chopped finely

3 garlic cloves, chopped

110 g/4 oz mushrooms, chopped into 1-cm/½-inch pieces

½ tbsp dark rum or wine

900 g/2 lb ground sirloin or the best ground beef you can get

1 tbsp Jerk Seasoning (see page 127, or Walkerwood ready-made) or less if you wish

2 tbsp chopped fresh parsley

1 tsp salt

½ tsp freshly ground pepper

To serve:

a few rocket sprigs per person (arugula)

6 tbsp Jerk Mustard (see page 129)

6 rolls, about 10 cm/4 inches long (use your favourite type of deli roll)

3 red onion slices, split into rings

1.   Place the butter in a saucepan and melt slowly. Add the onion, garlic and mushrooms and sauté for 3 minutes (do not allow to burn). De-glaze the pan with the rum or wine and allow to cook for 2 minutes more.

2.   Transfer the mushroom mixture to a large mixing bowl and mix in the beef, jerk seasoning and parsley. Season with salt and pepper. Form into 6 fat patties (about 3cm/1½ inches thick), place on a baking sheet, cover with cling film and allow to rest in the fridge for at least 30 minutes. (This can be done a day ahead.)

3.   Grill the burgers or fry them in a skillet for 5 minutes, on each side (medium rare).

4.   Cut the rolls in half and toast for about 2 minutes. Place a few sprigs of rocket on the bottom half of each bun, place each burger on this and top with a tablespoon of jerk mustard and a few rings of raw onion.

Cook's tip: For a different topping, place six cored pineapple slices under the grill, brush with melted butter and cook for 3–6 minutes on each side. Put on top of the rocket and lay your burger on top of this. Use a tbsp of Lime and Garlic Jerk Mayonnaise (see page 128) per person, instead of mustard, if you prefer.

Norma's Kingston Jerk Chicken

Norma Shirley is Executive Chef and owner of the Kingston-based Norma's On The Terrace, situated at the Jamaican landmark, Devon House. She has been described as the 'Julia Child of the Caribbean' and has a tremendous amount of international acclaim, having received numerous awards and features for fabulous cuisine, such as 'One of 60 Best New Restaurants in the World' (Condé Nast Traveler) 2002 and a culinary award from the Prime Minister of Jamaica.
Preparation and cooking time: marinating overnight + 40 minutes. Serves 6

6 chicken legs or 12 thighs, bone in

3 tbsp Jerk Seasoning (see page 127 or Walkerswood or Busha Brown ready-made)

4 tbsp finely chopped fresh chives or parsley, to garnish

For the vinaigrette:

225 ml/1 cup vegetable oil or extra virgin olive oil

90 ml/1/3 cup cane vinegar or distilled (white) malt vinegar

1 teaspoon Dijon mustard

1 tbsp lemon or lime juice

salt and pepper

For the caramelised fruit:

1 tbsp butter

1 tbsp sugar

6 slices of star fruit (carambola)

1. Add all the vinaigrette ingredients to a jar and shake until smooth. Taste and adjust the seasoning.

2. Mix the jerk seasoning with the vinaigrette in a bowl. Put the chicken pieces in it to marinate. Turn the pieces frequently. Cover and leave in the refrigerator to marinate for 6 hours or preferably overnight .

3. To make the caramelised fruit, heat the butter in a frying pan, add the sugar and melt. Add the slices of fruit and cook over a low heat for 5 minutes or until just soft and sticky. Set aside and re-warm just before chicken is done.

4. Turn on the grill. Remove the chicken from the marinade (reserve the marinade) and place on a baking sheet or in a roasting pan. Grill, basting with the marinade and turning the chicken frequently so as not to burn. Cook the chicken thoroughly, until the juices run clear when pierced with a skewer in the thickest part (about 40 minutes).

5. Set the chicken aside somewhere it remains warm. In a saucepan, place the remaining marinade and the drippings from the chicken and reduce to about 125 ml/1/2 cup of sauce.

6. Pour the sauce across a platter evenly. Place the chicken pieces on the sauce and garnish with the caramelised fruit slices and a sprinkle of chives or parsley.

Jerk Chicken Pasta

This is a continent away from the traditional use of jerk seasoning, but quick, easy and delicious. When drinking wine with a spicy meal like this, I recommend that you try something that's not too dry to work along with the robust flavours.
Preparation time: 1 hour marinating + 15 minutes cooking. Serves 4

6 skinless, boneless chicken thighs

1 tbsp Jerk Seasoning (see page 127, or Walkerswood ready-made)

450 g/1 lb penne or rigatoni

3 tbsp olive oil

1 onion, chopped

2–3 garlic cloves, chopped

60 ml/¼ cup red wine

4 plum tomatoes, skinned, de-seeded and chopped

1 cup tomato sauce

125 ml/¼ cup water or chicken stock

1 tbsp chopped fresh basil or parsley

salt and pepper

grated Romano or parmesan cheese, or crumbled feta cheese, to serve (optional)

1. Cut the chicken into strips. Rub thoroughly with the jerk seasoning, cover and let sit for at least 1 hour.

2. In a large pot, boil a gallon of water. Add 2 tsp salt and boil the pasta, stirring occasionally until al dente (about 11 minutes). Drain immediately in a large colander.

3. While the pasta water is boiling, heat 2 tbsp of the oil in a skillet. Fry the chicken pieces until browned. Add the onion and garlic and sauté for 2–3 minutes. (Do not allow garlic to burn).

4. De-glaze pan with red wine, scraping up slightly burned bits in the pan. Simmer for 1 minute and then add the tomatoes, tomato sauce, stock, salt and pepper. Simmer for 10 minutes. Check the seasoning (add a little water if needed).

5. In a large bowl, toss together the hot, drained pasta and chicken in tomato sauce and add the basil or parsley and remaining 1 tbsp of olive oil. Sprinkle with cheese if you like.

Jerk Cheese & Courgette Omelette

For some reason this is one of my top Sunday breakfast choices. Jerk cheese is now being produced in Jamaica and would work here very well.

Preparation and cooking time: 15 minutes. Serves 2

4 eggs
½ tsp Jerk Seasoning (see page 127, or Walkerswood dried jerk seasoning)
butter, for frying
½ small courgette, sliced thinly
½ cup grated mozzarella cheese, or use slices
salt and pepper

1. Beat the eggs and blend in the jerk seasoning.
2. Melt a little butter in a small single-omelette frying pan. As soon as it starts to bubble, add the courgette and allow to soften slightly for a few minutes. Season with salt and pepper. Remove from pan and reserve.
3. Add a little more butter to the pan, heat and then add the egg mixture. By tipping the pan you can make sure it covers the pan completely. Keep the heat low.
4. Using a spatula, break up the eggs as soon as they stick and allow some of the raw egg to seep through to the bottom. Do this once or twice, then layer on half the courgette and cheese in the middle of the egg.
5. When the egg seems almost firm, flip both sides towards the middle, covering the cheese. Turn the omelette once and cook for a few seconds. Though you want the cheese to melt, you don't want the eggs to dry out. Slide on to a plate and serve with toast.

Cook's tip: Use a mandoline to give you very thin vertical slices of courgette or use callaloo or spinach instead of courgette for your omelette filling.

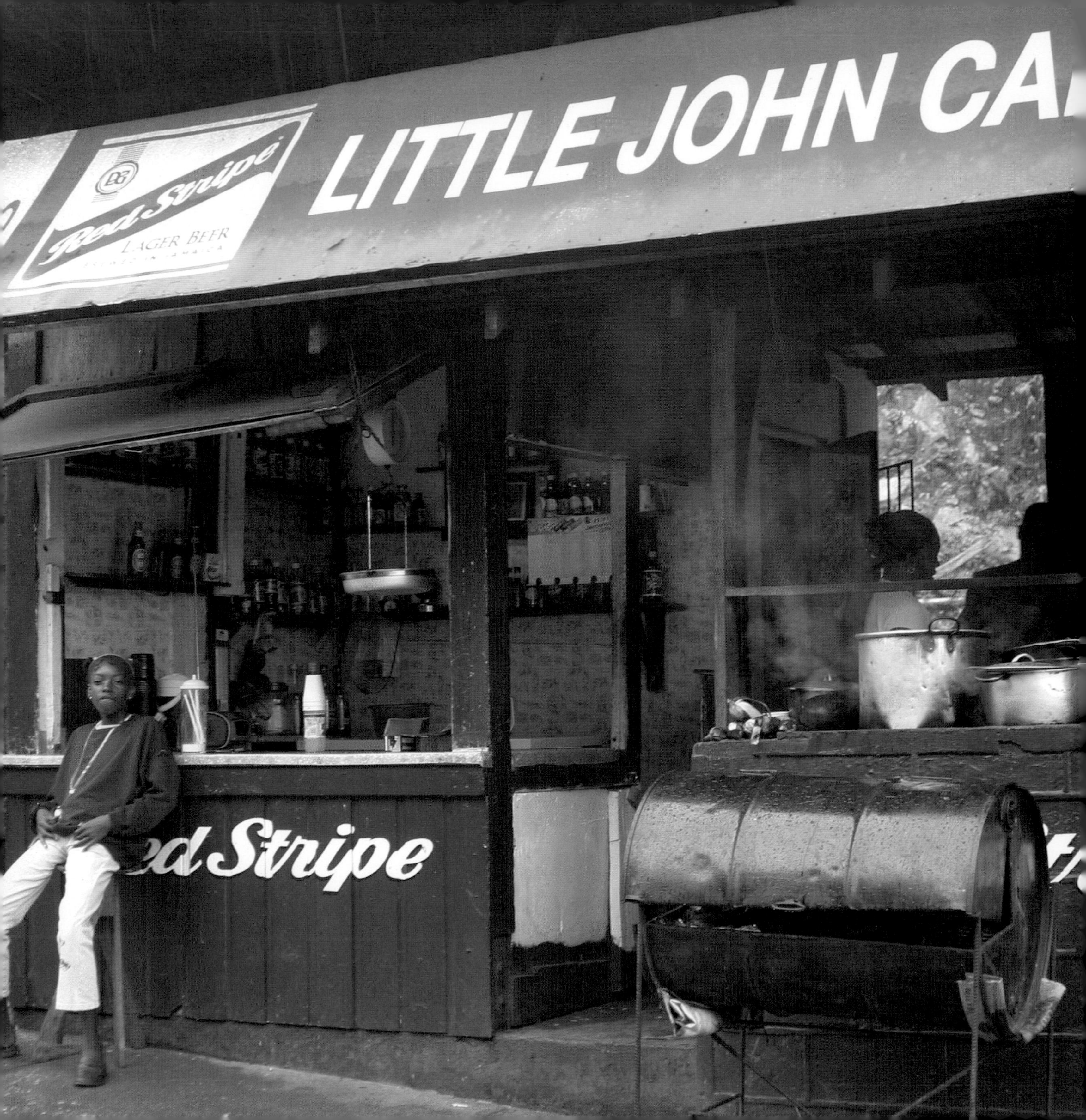

LITTLE JOHN CA
Red Stripe
LAGER BEER
ed Stripe

SUBSTANTIAL STEWS, GRILLS & SPICY ROASTS

It is difficult to generalise about the Caribbean islands. Though I have found many similarities amongst them, there are foods and practices that differ vastly. For instance, you'd be very hard pressed to find or convince anyone to eat blood sausage in Jamaica but it is a great favourite in Trinidad.

It is easy to rear a chicken, a few goats and a pig or two, but cattle-rearing requires pastureland and more sophisticated farming techniques. Only a few of the larger islands can support this. In Trinidad, a special breed of water buffalo has been bred for its meat ('buffalypso') but quite a lot of meat has to be imported into the Caribbean to satisfy the demand. Much of the beef and lamb you will find has been frozen.

Goat is eaten on many islands and is usually made into a stew, since it is very bony. Curried goat from Jamaica is almost legendary (see page 152). Lamb, which is a good substitute for goat, is reared in limited quantities and eaten in more upmarket environments. Pork is very popular on some islands, especially in Cuba and Puerto Rico, but for religious reasons it is more low profile and less popular in others.

Since the islanders who developed some of our best dishes were poor, you will find that little is wasted and there are delicious specialities made from what might have been left aside after the plantation owners had taken the choice bits. Some examples of these are Keshi Yena from Curaçao (see page 145), 'souse' (pickled pig's trotters) and 'cow foot', which is either done with beans or made as a jellied sweet. Liver and green bananas is a common breakfast but most other offal, like tripe and kidney, is more limited in popularity. I will mention oxtail, too, but that has been a favourite in the 'Great House' for a long time, along with pickled tongue. Pig's tail and salted beef are essentials in traditional soups and stews as they add huge flavour. For speed and convenience, islanders are using more seasoning powders and stock cubes but these not really a great substitute.

Most islanders like their meat well cooked; it is rare that you'll find a West Indian eating their meat rare. Personally, I adore steak tartare.

Keshi Yena
Curaçao

Keshi Yena is a traditional recipe from Curaçao. Literally translated, it means 'stuffed cheese'. The story goes that this dish was created from leftovers, on a Dutch plantation in Curaçao. A cook developed this use for the rind of the Edam cheese, which regularly ended up in the kitchen after the master's dinner. Serve with beans and rice and salad. This recipe was prepared for us by chef Michael Eseau in Curaçao.
Preparation time: 20 minutes + 25 minutes cooking time. Serves 6

2 tbsp oil

1 onion, chopped finely

2 garlic cloves, chopped finely

450 g/1 lb beef mince

2 tbsp piccalilli

2 tbsp roughly chopped pearl onions

2 tbsp sultanas

2 tbsp roughly chopped pimento-stuffed olives

2 tbsp roughly chopped pickled cucumbers

2 tbsp tomato purée

60 ml/¼ cup water

1 tbsp softened butter (to grease the ramekins)

450 g/1 lb Edam cheese, sliced thinly

1.   Heat the oil in a large saucepan, add the onion and garlic and fry for 5 minutes over moderate heat. Stir in the meat and continue frying for a further 5 minutes, or until the meat is browned all over. Drain off excess oil.

2.   Stir in the piccalilli, pearl onions, sultanas, stuffed olives, pickled cucumbers and tomato purée. Pour over the water and bring up to the boil. Reduce the heat and simmer for 10 minutes.

3.   Heat the oven to its highest setting. Grease six small ovenproof moulds, such as ramekins, with the butter. Line the moulds with slices of cheese, with some of the slices overlapping the top edge, to fold over the filling.

4.   Fill each mould with the beef mixture and fold over the overlapping cheese to cover. Pour some boiling water into a rectangular ovenproof dish and place the moulds inside the dish; the water should come halfway up the sides of the moulds. Place in the oven for 5–10 minutes, or until the cheese melts.

5.   Unmould the Keshi Yena by twisting the moulds, so that the cheese comes away from the sides. To do this place a clean cloth over the top and apply light pressure with the palm of your hand and twist. Then invert them on to a plate.

Pork Stuffed with Sweet Plantain, Served with Ajili-mojili (Hot Pepper & Garlic) Sauce

Puerto Rico

The combination of the sweet plantain stuffing with the succulent pork and a piquant 'ajili-mojili' sauce from Puerto Rico makes this an outstanding dish, full of contrasting flavours. For true garlic lovers! Ajili-mojili is traditionally served with bread.
Preparation time: marinating overnight + 20 minutes+ 1½ hours cooking. Serves 4–6

1½ tbsp adobo powder (see page 238, or ready-made)

1 kg /2 lb 2 oz boneless pork shoulder roll

1 ripe plantain, peeled and left whole

For the ajili-mojili sauce:

2 scotch bonnet peppers, de-seeded and chopped

6 whole peppercorns

6 garlic cloves

2 tsp salt

60 ml/¼ cup lime juice

2 tbsp cane vinegar or distilled (white) malt vinegar

125 ml/½ cup olive oil

1.   The day before, rub the adobo powder into the pork all over. Cover and place in the fridge overnight to marinate.

2.   Preheat the oven to 180°C/350°F/Gas Mark 4. The objective is to have the whole plantain centred in the roll of pork. If the cut of meat is solid at one end, slice a hole through so that the plantain can be shoved in and lined up in the centre of the cut. Roll and tie. Place in a roasting tray and roast, covered loosely with foil, for about an hour.

3.   Uncover and allow the roast to brown for a further 30–40 minutes, depending on how well done you like your pork. Don't overcook it or the meat will become dry. (A meat thermometer should read 170°F when it is done.)

4.   Meanwhile, as the meat is cooking, make the sauce. Place the hot pepper, peppercorns, garlic and salt in a blender and blend the ingredients until it forms a purée. Pour in the lime juice, vinegar and oil and blend again.

5.   Remove the pork from the oven and allow to stand for 10 minutes before carving. Serve with the ajili-mojili sauce handed around separately.

Oxtail with Riojà
Cuba

We ate this dish in a vibrant Cuban restaurant and were totally blown away by the delicious flavours. Serve it with the Sweet Plantain and Ginger Flans and Creamed Cassava with Roasted Garlic (see pages 179 and 180). It is a little time-consuming, but what a feast! In Jamaica we usually use a simpler method and stew the oxtail with broad beans.
Preparation time: marinating overnight + 25 minutes + 2 hours cooking. Serves 6

2 oxtails, cut into serving pieces, trimmed of excess fat

1–2 tbsp olive oil

2 garlic cloves, sliced

1 potato, cubed

2 onions, sliced

3 carrots, sliced

2 celery sticks, chopped

300 ml (½ pint) beef stock

300 ml (½ pint) water

750 ml (1 pint 5 fl oz) red Riojà wine

1 scotch bonnet pepper

2 bay leaves

1 tsp ground allspice

6 whole cloves

1 tbsp finely chopped fresh parsley, plus 1 tbsp to garnish

½ tsp ground nutmet

1 tbsp tomato purée

juice of 1 orange

1 teaspoon grated orange zest

For the seasoning:

2 garlic cloves, chopped

1 large onion, chopped

1 teaspoon fresh thyme leaves

salt and pepper

1. First of all blanch the oxtail, by pouring boiling water over it. Pat dry with kitchen paper. Combine the ingredients for the seasoning and season the meat, place in a bowl, cover and allow to marinate overnight in the fridge.

2. Heat the oil in a flameproof casserole, add the oxtail a few at a time and fry for 5–7 minutes or until the pieces are lightly browned. Remove with a slotted spoon and set aside in a bowl, while you fry the remaining pieces.

3. When all the meat is browned, add the garlic, potato, onions, carrots and celery to the casserole and sauté for 5 minutes, or until golden. Drain off any excess fat. Pour in the stock, water and 600 ml (1 pint) of the wine. Add the meat, the hot pepper, bay leaves, allspice, cloves, parsley, nutmeg, tomato purée, orange juice and orange zest. Season with salt and pepper.

4. Bring to the boil and then reduce the heat to low and simmer the oxtail for 1½–2 hours, or until the meat is soft and tender. (Remove the hot pepper before stirring as you don't want it to burst.)

5. To serve, transfer the meat to a warmed serving dish and set aside to keep warm whilst you make the sauce. Strain the juices through a sieve into another pan, pressing as much of the liquid as possible from the vegetables with the back of a wooden spoon. De-glaze the casserole with the remaining wine and then add to the sauce in the pan. Bring to the boil; remove from the heat and pour over the oxtail. Serve immediately, sprinkled with the remaining parsley.

Beef Stew with Pimento & Rum

This dish is quite traditional in both technique and flavour. The rum element is very mild. The quality of meat will dictate the cooking time. Feel free to add a few carrots if you like.

Preparation time: 1 hour marinating + 15 minutes + 2 hours cooking. Serves 6

1.3 kg/3 lb braising steak, cubed	about 2–3 tbsp oil, for browning
1½ tbsp ground allspice	600 ml/1 pint beef stock
1 tsp salt	150 ml/¼ pint dark rum
freshly ground black pepper	1 bay leaf
2 garlic cloves, chopped	2 whole cloves
2 large onions, sliced	1 tbsp tomato purée
2 tbsp Pickapeppa Sauce (use Worcestershire Sauce as a substitute)	2 tsp brown sugar
	3 potatoes, peeled and cubed
2 tbsp flour	1 tbsp chopped fresh parsley or chives, to garnish

1.	Season the meat with allspice, salt, pepper, garlic, onions and Pickapepper or Worcestershire sauce. Allow to marinate for an hour at least. Preheat the oven to 180°C/350°F/Gas Mark 4.

2.	Brush the seasoning off the meat and reserve it. Dust the meat with the flour and shake off excess.

3.	Put some oil in a large ovenproof skillet (with cover) and heat on stove top. Brown the meat in batches for about 10 minutes each time. Then return all the meat to the pot with the reserved seasonings. De-glaze the pan with half the rum, making sure to scrape off the sticky bits on the bottom. Then stir in the stock, adding the bay leaf, cloves, tomato purée and brown sugar. Place in the oven and cook for an hour.

4.	Stir and check how tender the meat is. Add the potatoes to the stew (and carrots if you wish). Cover and continue to braise until meat is tender, which could be from 30 minutes to 1 hour, keeping an eye on the liquid. Remove from oven.

5.	Place on stovetop on low heat and stir in the remainder of the rum. Simmer for 2 minutes. Taste the sauce and adjust the seasoning. Garnish with the parsley or chives.

Cook's tip: I have also used beef tenderloin and done the whole dish on the stovetop in half the time. Your only adjustment is to use about 150 ml/¼ pint less stock (as there is not so much time for reduction). Cut the potatoes smaller so they cook and thicken the gravy faster otherwise you will be tempted to use cornflour, which will dull the flavour at bit.

Colombo de Cabri (Goat Curry)

Guadaloupe

'Colombo' is a special mixture of Indian spices used for making a curry dish in the French Antilles. It was brought to the island originally in the nineteenth century from Sri Lanka. The spices used in colombo powder vary but it is basically a kind of garam masala. Use your favourite curry powder if you can't find colombo. In Jamaica, where 'curried goat' is a daily favourite, the method is similar: just leave out the aubergines and cloves. *Preparation time: marinating overnight + 20 minutes + 2¼ hours cooking. Serves 6–8*

1.5 kg/3½ lb boneless lean goat meat, washed, dried
    and cut into cubes (2 kg/4.5 lb with bone)

a bunch of fresh chives, chopped

5 garlic cloves, 4 crushed 1 reserved

a small bunch of fresh thyme, leaves chopped

1 scotch bonnet pepper, de-seeded and chopped

3 tbsp colombo, garam masala or (preferably West
    Indian) curry powder

4 tbsp vegetable oil

4 whole cloves

4 aubergines, cut into chunks

1 litre/1¾ pints water

salt and pepper

juice of 1 lime, to serve

1.   First of all season the goat meat with half the chives, crushed garlic and thyme, the scotch bonnet pepper and half of the colombo, garam masala or curry powder. Set aside for several hours or overnight to marinate.

2.   Heat the oil in a large flameproof casserole or 'dutchie', add a little of the meat at a time and brown to seal. When it is done, add the remaining crushed garlic and cook for a few minutes, and then rest of the chives and thyme and the cloves.

3.   Add the aubergines and remaining spice powder and mix all the ingredients well together in the pot. Pour over the water and bring to the boil. Reduce the heat to low, season with salt and pepper, cover the pot and cook for 1½–2 hours or until the meat is tender. Stir occasionally and add more water to keep liquid in the pot. This will make a nice rich gravy along with the meat.

4.   Just as you turn off the heat, squeeze over the juice of ½–1 lime and sprinkle on the last clove of garlic, finely chopped. Stir in and serve.

Cook's tip: The term masala means 'spices'; 'garam masala' is mixed spice. To make your own, take 1 tbsp cardamom seeds, 1 tsp cumin seeds, 1 tsp whole cloves, 1 tsp black peppercorns, ½ tsp grated nutmeg, a 5-cm/2-inch cinnamon stick and ½ tsp cayenne or dried chilli. Place them all in a grinder and grind as finely as possible. Store in an airtight container for a week or two.

Picadillo Pie topped with Sweet Potato
Cuba

Ground-beef hash or 'picadillo' as it is known in Cuba is traditionally served with a fried egg on top. Taking a bit of licence here, I've turned the basic recipe into a spicy filling for a sweet potato 'shepherd's pie'. This way you'll get a tummy-warming one-pot meal.
Preparation time: 45 minutes + 20 minutes cooking. Serves 6

2 tbsp oil

2 onions, minced

700 g/1½ lb ground beef

1 scotch bonnet pepper, de-seeded and minced or 1 tsp Jerk
   Seasoning (see page 127, or Walkerswood ready-made)

2 garlic cloves, crushed

1 sweet pepper (red or green), de-seeded and chopped

4 tomatoes, peeled and chopped

2 tbsp minced fresh parsley

½ tsp cumin seeds

2 tsp dried oregano

¼ tsp ground cloves

2 tbsp golden raisins

1 tsp salt

3 tbsp chopped stuffed green olives

2 tbsp capers, rinsed (optional)

salt

freshly ground black pepper

For the topping:

4 sweet potatoes, peeled and boiled

1 tbsp butter

70 ml/¼ cup milk

¼ tsp ground allspice

1.   Preheat the oven to 180°C/350°F/Gas Mark 4. Put the sweet potatoes in a pan of salted water and boil until tender, about 20 minutes. Drain well.

2.   Meanwhile, heat the oil in a large heavy-bottomed skillet. Add the onions and cook over medium heat for about 6 minutes until soft.

3.   Add the meat and cook, stirring constantly, for about 10 minutes or until lightly coloured.

4.   Add the hot pepper, garlic, green or red pepper, tomatoes, parsley, cumin, oregano, cloves, golden raisins, salt and pepper and cook for 3 minutes, stirring frequently.

5.   Stir in the chopped olives and capers and cook for a further few minutes. Taste and adjust the seasoning. Put into a casserole dish, leaving space for the sweet potato topping.

6.   Mash the sweet potatoes with the butter and milk and season with allspice. Put this on top of the picadillo and spread evenly. Place in the hot oven for 20 minutes or until the potato topping starts to brown on the edges.

HEALTHY, HEARTY HOT POTS

Essential to any good meal is the balance of flavours, colour, texture and nutrition. This is never more so than with vegetarian dishes.

I was first introduced to the concept of vegetarianism through a friend's mother. She ate only vegetables and cheese from what I could detect. She couldn't cook. What she did cook she boiled to death in very salty water, it was her seasoning and her finishing sauce. I admit it made me a bit sceptical of all vegetarians for a while.

It wasn't until years later – when I met Bob Marley and was introduced to the Rastafarian cooking pot – that I realised that due to my early misconceptions about vegetarianism and constant years of masking flavours with too much salt I had been missing a world of vegetarian subtlety. I now love vegetarian food and will quite happily do without a meat course if the vegetarian replacement is delicious.

Stuffed Christophene

A delicious starter, side dish or main vegetarian course. Christophenes (cho-chos) are usually eaten steamed with butter or in soups. They are great in salads, raw, but that is not a traditional use. They are popular stuffed with meat, but we won't discuss that in this chapter.

Preparation and cooking time: about 1 hour. Serves 2 as a main course or 4 as a side dish

2 christophenes

1 tbsp butter

1 spring onion, chopped

2 slices of fresh white bread, trimmed and whizzed into crumbs

¼ tsp grated nutmeg

a dash of hot pepper sauce

75 g/¾ cup grated Cheddar cheese

salt and pepper

1. Cut the christophenes in two lengthways, place in a pot of boiling, salted water and cook until tender. Remove from the heat, drain and leave to cool.

2. Sauté the chopped spring onion in butter until softened. Then add the breadcrumbs and fry until brown.

3. Scoop the seed and coarse centre vein out of the christophenes and discard. Scoop out the rest of the flesh and add to the breadcrumb mixture. Make sure not to damage the skin as you will need to stuff it.

4. Keeping the mixture on a low heat, mix in the nutmeg, hot sauce and salt and pepper to taste. Add half of the cheese and mix well.

5. Stuff the christophene shells with the warm mix and top with the rest of the cheese.

6. Place under a hot grill until the cheese starts to brown. Serve hot.

Cook's tip: Do not ask 'cho-chos' outside of Jamaica as it means quite something else in Spanish.

I-tal Curry

This is a basic vegetable curry, West Indian style. In keeping with Rastafarian tradition you might wish to try it without salt. Don't use anything canned, either, as you want the purest, freshest food. Remember, 'I-tal is vital' so get started grating that coconut.

Preparation and cooking time: 40 minutes. Serves 4–6

For the vegetables:

450 g/1 lb potatoes (about 2 medium potatoes)

450 g/1 lb sweet potatoes

350 g/12 oz peeled and de-seeded pumpkin

½ small green cabbage

1 large carrot

1 red, green or yellow sweet pepper, de-seeded

½ cauliflower

225 g/8 oz green beans or bodi (runner beans)

1 scotch bonnet pepper, de-seeded and chopped

For the seasoning:

2 tbsp vegetable oil

1 spring onion

1 tsp fresh thyme leaves

1 onion, chopped

6 allspice berries

2 garlic cloves, chopped

2 tsp curry powder

125–225 ml/½–1 cup coconut milk

1 tsp garam masala (see Cook's tip page 154), to serve (optional)

1. Cut all the vegetables into 2.5-cm/1-inch pieces.

2. Heat the oil in a large skillet, add the spring onion, thyme, onion, allspice, garlic and curry. Keep stirring until lightly browned.

2. Add coconut milk, depending on amount of vegetables and to your taste, and mix in. Add the potatoes. Allow to cook for about 5 minutes.

3. Add the rest of the vegetables and hot pepper to taste. Lower the heat and simmer, covered, for another 5–10 minutes, until the vegetables are just cooked. Add water at any time if needed, but only enough to prevent sticking. Sprinkle on the garam masala at the end.

Cook's tip: Basically you can use virtually any choice of your favourite vegetables.

Stuffed Aubergine with Curried Rice

If you use large aubergines, a half will do for each person as a main vegetarian course. Smaller aubergines make a good side dish.

Preparation time: 15 minutes de-gorging + 45 minutes + 35 minutes cooking. Serves 4 as a main course

2 large aubergines

1 cup white long-grain rice

olive oil, for frying

1 large onion, chopped

2 garlic cloves minced

2 tsp chopped fresh thyme

4 tsp curry powder

4 tbsp coconut powder, mixed with 60 ml/¼ cup water, or 60 ml/¼ cup canned coconut milk

2 large tomatoes de-seeded and chopped

4 tbsp chopped fresh coriander

salt and pepper

1. Cut the aubergine lengthways and scoop out the insides but don't go too close to the skins as you'll need them intact for stuffing. Use a metal measuring spoon to scoop as it is often sharp. Put aside.
2. Sprinkle the aubergine flesh with salt and leave for about 15 minutes to remove bitterness and any loose seeds. Rinse and drain. Pat dry with kitchen paper. Preheat the oven to 180°C/350°F/Gas Mark 4.
3. Meanwhile, cook the rice according to instructions.
4. Heat some oil in large skillet and sauté the onion, garlic, thyme and curry powder for a few minutes until the onion is translucent. Add the chopped aubergine flesh and cook, stirring occasionally. As soon as the aubergine softens, add the coconut milk. Cover and simmer for about 8 minutes. Season to taste.
5. Add the tomato, coriander and rice and mix together.
6. Stuff the aubergine skins with the mixture and bake on a greased baking sheet for 30–35 minutes, until just browned.

Cook's tip: This is a good way to use up leftover rice.

Caribbean Vegetable Stir-fry with Coconut Noodles

The strategy for stir-frying is to cut the vegetables into similar, bite-sized pieces, to cook them in the right order (hardest first, as these will take longest to cook) and to keep the heat hot and the pieces moving in the wok. Try to time the noodles so they don't have to sit around for too long.

Preparation and cooking time: 50 minutes. Serves 4–6

450 g/1 lb Hokkien, Ramen or any Chinese noodles

2–4 tbsp oil, for frying

225 g/8 oz peeled and de-seeded pumpkin, cut into 1-cm/½-inch cubes

1 ripe plantain, cut into 1-cm/½-inch cubes

175 g/6 oz green beans, topped, tailed and halved

2 carrots, julienned

1 onion, cut into 8 wedges, layers separated

110 g/4 oz white or green cabbage, chopped

1 red sweet pepper, julienned

½ tbsp minced fresh root ginger

1 garlic clove, chopped

225 ml/1 cup coconut milk

1 tbsp chilli oil

½ cup chopped cashew nuts

1. Boil the noodles in a pan of salted, boiling water according to the instructions. (Keep warm.)
2. Heat 2 tbsp of cooking oil in a wok. When it is really hot, carefully drop in the pumpkin and then the plantain cubes. Stir-fry carefully until tender (it takes a few in minutes and you need to give it constant attention) and then push them to the side.
3. Then drop the green beans in the middle. As they cook, push up to the sides and add the carrots. These all need to be cooked through, though not overcooked.
4. Add a little more oil to the wok (if necessary) and bring back to heat. Follow with the rest of the vegetables, stirring until everything is lightly cooked yet still brightly coloured and crunchy. Add the coconut milk.
5. Drain the noodles and toss with the vegetables. Drizzle over the chilli oil, add the nuts and toss again. Serve right away.

Summer Ackee Pasta

Jamaica

Far from traditional, pasta is nevertheless becoming popular in the Caribbean. Ackee, that curious fruit from Jamaica, is an unique vegetarian treat. It combines well with pasta and cheese. Since ackees are very delicate, be gentle when you mix them in. This is called a summer pasta because the tomatoes and seasonings remain uncooked.

Preparation and cooking time: 20 minutes. Serves 6

4–6 plum tomatoes, de-seeded and chopped (fresh is essential)

1 spring onion, sliced finely diagonally

1–2 garlic cloves, pressed or chopped very finely

1/2 tsp chopped fresh thyme leaves

1/2 scotch bonnet pepper, de-seeded and chopped finely (optional)

3–4 tbsp olive oil (extra virgin or the best you can find)

550 g/1 1/4 lb ackees, cleaned, or 560 g can of ackees, drained

450 g/1 lb fusilli, farfalle or penne (pasta twists, bows or quills)

a large handful of fresh basil, coriander or parsley, torn into pieces

50 g/2 oz freshly grated parmesan cheese or crumbled feta cheese (optional)

salt and pepper

1. In a large ceramic or glass bowl, combine the tomatoes, spring onion, garlic, thyme, scotch bonnet, salt and pepper with 2 tbsp of the oil.

2. Cook the cleaned, yellow part of the ackees (if using fresh) in boiling, salted water for about 10 minutes until just tender. Remove from heat and drain. Otherwise, just heat canned ackees in their brine and drain before using.

3. Cook the pasta in a large pan of rapidly boiling, salted water until al dente. Then drain in a large colander.

4. Add the steaming pasta immediately to the tomato mixture and toss with some of the remaining oil. Season with salt and pepper. Add the ackees, the basil or other herbs and your choice of cheese, if using, and toss again. Serve immediately, with a fresh green salad.

Cook's tip: There are several variations on this dish which are equally delicious, including the addition of 1/2 cup prepared salt fish or 1/2 cup olives.

Use coloured pasta for a little extra visual excitement: try green (spinach), red (tomato) or black (squid ink) pasta.

Baked Aubergine with Callaloo Rundown

Jamaica

In Jamaica we can buy freshly picked callaloo in bundles at the roadside and one bundle would be perfect for this dish; but if that's difficult for you (maybe on your next visit) you could buy a can or two of cooked callaloo and drain off the water. Another option is to use spinach which is also a part of the leafy green family. This is a hearty vegetable dish.

Preparation time: 30 minutes de-gorging + 20 minutes + 40 minutes cooking. Serves 4–6

450 g/1 lb aubergine (about 2 medium), sliced 5 mm/¼ inch thick

1 bundle of fresh callaloo or spinach or a 19 oz/538 g can of callaloo, or frozen spinach, thawed

2 tbsp olive oil

2 tsp chopped fresh rosemary

2 garlic cloves, minced

1 onion, chopped

6 small plum tomatoes, skinned, de-seeded and chopped

300 ml/½ pint coconut milk

oil, for frying

For the topping:

2 tomatoes, sliced

chopped fresh rosemary

salt and pepper

1. Slice the aubergines, place in a bowl, sprinkle liberally with salt and leave to sit for half an hour. Preheat the oven to 180°C/350°F/Gas Mark 4.

2. Prepare the fresh callaloo by stripping the coarse outer skin on the stalks (much like with celery), and then chopping the stalks and leaves and steaming in just the water clinging to the leaves after washing, until just wilted. Cook spinach in the same way. Or simply drain a can of callaloo or the defrosted spinach.

3. When the aubergine is ready, discard the bitter juices now collected in the bowl, rinse off the excess salt and drain thoroughly. Mix the oil, rosemary and garlic and pour over the aubergine, ensuring everything gets a little coating.

4. Heat a little oil in a skillet and sautè the aubergine over low heat for about 10 minutes, covered, until just softening. Remove from pan and set aside.

5. Put a little more oil in the skillet and sauté the onions until translucent. Add the tomatoes and callaloo or spinach. Sprinkle with salt and pepper. When warm, add the coconut milk and stir together.

6. Make a layer of half the aubergine at the base of an casserole dish. Pour in the callaloo mixture and then layer again with the rest of the aubergine. Top with overlapping slices of tomato, brush with oil and sprinkle with salt, pepper and rosemary. Bake for about 40 minutes.

Strict Rastafarians don't eat meat, especially pork, as like Jews and Moslems, they adhere to the tenets of the Old Testament (Leviticus) and the Qur'an that forbid eating swine because they are unclean scavengers.

A Bob Story Rastafarians are a religious group, originating in Jamaica, with beliefs based on the Bible. They follow the direct lineage of Emperor Haile Selassie of Ethiopia from the union of Solomon and Sheba – hence the Ethiopian flag, Star of David and images of the Conquering Lion of Judah in their visual representations. They go a step further and scratch salt from their diet too – this cuisine is known as 'I-tal food' and takes a little getting used to. The word I-tal is similar to 'vital' and the food should be pure, without chemicals, preservatives, cans or processing.

Bob Marley is probably the best known Rastafarian and he and his reggae band, The Wailers, would not have dreamed of going on the road without their cook, Mikey Dan.

I-tal food is prepared with organic grains like oats for porridge, brown rice, tofu, beans, groundnuts, ground provisions, lentils, cabbage, chayote, callaloo, carrots, pak choy and sometimes fish (but no scavenging shellfish) and it is flavoured a lot with coconut milk, peppers and seasoning herbs. Honey and cinnamon are popular for use in porridge and sweets.

I have a little admission to make here. I talked Bob into going to a friend's restaurant in London years ago and, by some freakish mistake, ordered myself a pork dish (which for him, would have been totally sacrilegious). I ate the whole thing in front of him. I later found out – and you'd have to have been around at the time to understand – how scorned I might have been, which is why I've never admitted this before. Respect.

GROUND PROVISIONS, RICE, BREADS & PLANTAINS

Crispy, chewy bammies (cassava cakes), steaming buttery yams, sticky dumplings: these are the dishes which support the main course and add a lot of character to our cuisine. In the Orient either rice or noodles are prepared daily; in Europe and America the preference tends towards breads, potatoes and pasta. In the Caribbean we have a range of ground provisions (foodstuffs grown in the ground), sometimes referred to as 'blue food', because some, such as coco and yampie, have a blueish-purple tinge when cooked. These are usually boiled and placed beside the meat to sop up the gravy.

These starches play a huge part in the Caribbean diet. I know how awkward a plate of boiled green bananas, hunks of yellow yam and a fat grey dumpling might appear to someone who is unaccustomed but I could not bear to eat many of our traditional dishes without these staples. There is something about the earthy blandness which is comforting. For the unconverted, however, I know I need to compromise here, and maybe introduce these dishes a little at a time while working on the appearance a bit, so I am presenting these items in more refined versions.

Up to a few years ago, the only noodles around here were in macaroni and cheese or in Chinese food. The Caribbean has now adopted pasta and, though still a relatively upmarket dish, it has been embraced enthusiastically by athletes (for energy) and by younger people who have been exposed through their travels and recognise the ease of the trendy pasta dish.

Rice, flour and cornmeal are at the heart of every kitchen and potatoes are sometimes simply referred to simply as 'Irish'. Often we add vegetables to plain rice to jazz it up. For example, 'pumpkin rice' is just a matter of cubing small pieces of pumpkin and adding them to rice before steaming. Or try 'callaloo rice', which is cooked with the beloved coconut milk and a cup or so of chopped callaloo. Don't forget to add salt to the boiling water and, to wake up plain rice, add a dash of your favourite mixed spices or some curry or annatto oil for colour.

Plantains, though technically a fruit (the big cousin of the banana), are eaten as a starch, side dish or snack and they are consumed on every island. Used at every stage, from green to very ripe, they come in various sizes.

The first thing you should know about a plantain is that no matter at what stage of ripeness you choose yours, they must be cooked before consuming. They are very slippery when raw, but lose this once cooked.

Plantains are available anywhere there is a hub of West Indian, Hispanic or African patrons. I have noticed that supermarkets tend to remove the ripe but blackening plantains, maybe thinking that, like bananas, they have passed their sell-by date. No, those are ready for frying tonight! Leave them though, if they have reached the stage of growing mould.

To cut a plantain, trim the ends off and then slit the skin from top to tail, trying not to cut through the flesh. Peel back by getting a finger under the skin and pulling it back all in one piece (it won't divide into three peels like a banana). For a very green plantain you might want to slit it twice and pull the pieces off bit by bit with your fingers, much as you would an orange. They are served whole, in chunks, rings, slices or mashed and there are many ways to prepare them.

Fried Ripe Plantain Take a plantain which is quite ripe, peel and slice diagonally, each slice about 8–10 mm (1/3–1/2 inch) thick. Sometimes they are cut in strips horizontally but they can be quite slippery, making cutting like that a bit harder. The most important thing is, don't slice too thinly.

Drop into hot oil and turn once or twice until the colour changes and the edges are crispy brown. Place on kitchen paper to blot excess oil. They become an orange colour and inside will be soft but firm.

Baked Ripe Plantain People often fry plantains while a tad too young, when they are not yet fully sweet – those will be better baked.

Choose a ripe one. Remove the skin. You can dot with butter or brush with oil and wrap whole in foil and bake on the oven rack along with roasts or set it whole beside your chicken in the pan about 15 minutes before the chicken's done (earlier if the plantain is not very ripe). It will crisp up on the outside in the chicken fat.

Or you can cut in two and slice again, horizontally in two. Place sliced sides down in a greased casserole dish, pour over the juice of one orange (per plantain), sprinkle on a little ground cinnamon and a tsp of grated orange zest and bake in a moderate oven (180°C/350°F/Gas Mark 4) for 20 minutes. You can even add a spoon or two of honey or guava jelly if you really like them sweet. This is still regarded as a side dish – not a dessert.

Tostones (Twice-fried Green Plantain) Pull the skin off and slice in 1-cm/½-inch rounds. If it is a really big plantain you'll get about 16–18 slices. Soak for a few minutes in cold salted water and then pat dry before you drop them in hot oil. Turn when just golden. Remove, absorb excess oil on kitchen paper and then smash them with a rolling pin or a press (you don't want to destroy the slices, just flatten them). Then drop them in hot oil again and fry until golden. Remove and place on kitchen paper once more. This time they will be fantastically crispy. Sprinkle with salt. They deserve to be eaten while still warm. Serve with a sprinkling of minced garlic in oil if you like.

Mashed Green or Semi-ripe Plantain Trim the ends and slit the skin as before but this time you can cut the plantain in two and drop into boiling water with the skin on. (You can do the same with green bananas.) Boil for about 10–15 minutes until a fork goes in easily (like with a potato). The skin will come off magically. Drain, remove skin and mash the flesh with butter and milk. Season this with salt and freshly ground pepper. Serve as you would mashed potatoes.

Festival

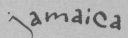

A slightly sweet and very moreish fried dumpling from Jamaica, traditionally served with jerk meats.
Preparation time: 10 minutes + 10 minutes cooking. Serves 6

125 g/1 cup cornmeal
125 g/1 cup plain flour
1 tsp baking powder
1 tbsp sugar
½ tsp salt
enough cold water for mixing a soft dough
oil, for frying

1. Mix all the dry ingredients together in a bowl.
2. Add just enough cold water to make a stiff dough. Flour your hands.
3. Knead it lightly and divide into 12 portions. Roll these into a small log or cigar shape and pinch a few times to flatten slightly.
4. Pour enough oil into a skillet to reach about 2.5-cm/1-inch deep and put over fairly high heat. Just as the oil begins to smoke, carefully slide in the dumplings and fry and turn for about 8 minutes, turning until golden brown on both sides. Drain on kitchen paper.

Hot Pepper Bread

This light pepper bread is both sweet and hot. You can vary the amount of hot pepper you wish to include, depending to your taste. Serve with soup or fish dishes.

Preparation time: 15 minutes activating yeast + 30 minutes + 4 hours total proving + 40 minutes baking. Makes 2 loaves

17 g sachet dried active yeast

225 ml/1 cup lukewarm water

2 tbsp sugar

2 eggs, lightly beaten, plus 1 beaten egg for glazing

1 tsp salt

2 tbsp vegetable oil, plus 1 tbsp for oiling bowl

500 g/1 lb 2 oz strong white flour, plus extra for kneading

½ each, red, yellow and green sweet peppers, de-seeded and finely chopped

2–4 scotch bonnet peppers (depending on how much heat you can take!), de-seeded and chopped finely

1. Mix the yeast, water and sugar together in a large bowl. Cover and leave for 10–15 minutes, or until it froths and bubbles appear on the surface.

2. Beat the eggs, salt and vegetable oil into the yeast mixture until thoroughly combined and then add the flour and peppers, working them in slowly.

3. Sprinkle some flour on to your work surface and then knead the dough for 5–10 minutes until it is very smooth and elastic. If the dough is too sticky, add more flour.

4. Lightly oil the bowl and return the dough, turning it so that it is completely covered in oil. Cover the bowl and set aside in a warm place to rise for 2–3 hours, or until it has doubled in size.

5. Punch down the dough and divide it in half. Form into two round loaves. Place on a non-stick baking sheet. Cover and set aside for 1 hour, until doubled in size.

6. Preheat the oven to 190°C/375°F/Gas Mark 6. Brush the tops with the remaining egg and bake in the centre of the oven for 30–40 minutes, or until the loaves are a golden brown. To test if they are done, turn them over and tap the bottoms; they should sound hollow. Leave to cool on a wire rack.

Coconut Bake
Trinidad

Serve this crumbly light Trinidadian coconut bake for breakfast with Bul Jol or Pick-up Saltfish (see page 47).

Preparation time: 10 minutes + 1 hour proving + 30 minutes baking. Makes a 30-cm/12-inch round loaf

450 g/1 lb plain flour

3 tsp baking powder

½ tsp salt

2 tbsp brown sugar

60 g/2 oz grated coconut

100 g/4 oz butter

40 g/1½ oz lard or white vegetable
shortening

300 ml/½ pint coconut milk

1. Preheat the oven to 180°C/350°F/Gas Mark 4. Grease a baking sheet.

2. Sift the flour, baking powder and salt into a bowl. Add the brown sugar and grated coconut and then rub in the butter and lard or shortening.

3. Slowly add the coconut milk and mix together to form a dough. Knead for 5 minutes until the dough is smooth. Leave to rest for 1 hour.

4. Shape into a ball and roll out to a disc 2.5-cm/1-inch thick. Place on the greased baking sheet and bake for 20–30 minutes or until golden and the bottom sounds hollow when tapped.

Mini Tortillas

Tortilla is a traditional spanish potato omelette, which is sliced and eaten at room temperature and therefore particularly good for lunch picnics or cold buffets.

I have taken a little licence here and made mini ones, and added some calalloo and cheese and this and that. Have some fun mixing your layers and combinations in each cup and feel free to try some new flavours as you get a taste for it.

The object is to fill each cup with potato, onion and batter. Add layers of cheese or calalloo as you wish and sprinkle any spices you like, but go lightly as the whole point of a tortilla is a fairly bland bit of comfort food.

Preparation time: 30 minutes + 45 minutes cooking. Makes 12

2 onions, sliced in rings, rings cut in half
1 tbsp butter
Options:
225 g/8 oz potatoes grated coarsely
225 g/8 oz sweet potatoes grated, coarsely
1/2 cup grated cheese
1/2 cup cooked callaloo, greens or spinach
cayenne, chilli powder, curry powder, garlic powder, oregano or paprika
For the basic batter:
8 eggs, beaten
125 ml/1/2 cup cream
1 tsp salt
1/4 tsp black pepper
pinch of freshly grated nutmeg

1. Preheat the oven to 180°C/350°F/Gas Mark 4.
2. Grease a 12 hole muffin tin well.
3. Whisk the batter ingredients together. This is enough to fill all the cups along with the fillings. I find that a 'turkey baster' is ideal for filling the cups with batter.
4. Sauté the onion in the butter, until soft.
5. Place a layer of potato and then a layer of onion in the muffin tin holes and pour in some batter. Then add a layer of cheese, then more potato and top with more batter and a sprinkle of chilli powder. *That was an example of one cup.* Make up your own combos, using up the ingredients and flavouring with spices to suit.
6. When all the compartments are full, place in oven for 25–30 minutes, until done. Cool before turning out. Serve as a side dish.

Sweet Plantain & Ginger Flans

These sweet and savoury flans make the perfect accompaniment to our delicious Oxtail in Riojà (see page 149). In fact they will go well with any rich stew, meat or game.

Preparation and cooking time: 40 minutes. Serves 6

4 sweet, ripe plantains

5-cm/2-inch piece of fresh root ginger, peeled and grated

4 eggs, beaten

300 ml/½ pint milk

½ tsp ground cinnamon

1 tbsp butter

salt and freshly ground black pepper

1. Preheat the oven to 180°C/350°F/Gas Mark 4.

2. Top and tail the plantains, slit down one side with a sharp knife and peel off the skins. Boil for about 10–15 minutes.

3. Remove from the heat, drain and transfer to a mixing bowl. Using a potato masher, mash them to a pulp. Stir in the ginger, eggs and milk and then season with the cinnamon, salt and pepper.

4. Grease six ramekin dishes with the butter and spoon in the mixture. Place in a roasting tin and pour in some boiling water, (making sure none spills in the mixture). The water should come halfway up the sides of the dishes. Place in the oven and cook for 15 minutes, or until the flans are firm to the touch.

5. Carefully remove the roasting tin from the heat. Remove the ramekin dishes and serve by inverting them on to individual dishes.

Roasted Breadfruit

You can make this on a stovetop gas fire or on a coal-pot or barbecue. What you need is a low, open fire. Choose a semi-ripe breadfruit, not a soft one. If you have any leftovers, see Fried Roasted Breadfruit (page 48).
Preparation time: 1 hour cooking + 15 minutes cooling and peeling. Makes about 16 slices

1 semi-ripe breadfruit
butter

1. Cut out the stem of the breadfruit and place stem-down on a medium fire. Keep turning until evenly charred on all sides.
2. You should finish with the stem up and the whole breadfruit blackened. When it is done (about 45–60 minutes), steam should be seen coming out of the opening. A knife pushed in should come out clean.
3. Allow to cool just enough to be handled and peel off the charred skin. You'll be left with a cream-coloured ball. Cut in two and then into quarters and remove the core. Proceed to slice in wedges and serve immediately, with butter.

Creamed Cassava with Roasted Garlic

This dish rates as utterly delicious comfort food. It makes a fantastic substitute at a time when you might have chosen just mashed potatoes. It's no sweat.
Preparation and cooking time: 20 minutes. Serves 6

1 kg/2 lb 4 oz cassava, peeled and cut into cubes	**300 ml/½ pint warm milk**
1 whole head of garlic	**grated nutmeg**
60 g/2 oz butter	**salt and freshly ground black pepper**

1. Preheat the oven to 190°C/375°F/Gas Mark 6. Place the cassava in large saucepan, cover with water, add 1 tsp of salt and bring to the boil. Reduce the heat to low, cover the pan and simmer for 20 minutes, or until the cassava is cooked and soft.
2. Meanwhile, place the head of garlic in the oven and bake for 20 minutes or until soft. Remove from the oven and set aside.
3. Remove the cassava from the heat, strain and put back into the pan. Using a potato masher, mash the cassava until it is smooth. Using a fork, beat in the butter and milk. Squeeze the garlic pulp out of the skins and add to the cassava. Mix well together with the fork, season with nutmeg, salt and freshly ground pepper and serve immediately.

Rice & Peas

Jamaica

There is probably no dish more popular from island to island, in all its varieties, than rice and peas. Sometimes they are prepared separately, as in yellow rice and red beans or Cuban style 'Moros y Cristianos' (black beans and white rice) or all together as in Trinidadian 'peas and rice' or Jamaican 'rice and peas'. On the French islands like Haiti it is known as 'riz et pois colles'. The seasonings vary slightly, as does use of coconut milk, meat stock or spices for cooking the beans and peas. Because of the lengthy cooking time for beans, it is often a weekend speciality but many islanders use a pressure cooker to make it faster.

Popular beans for this Jamaican dish are kidney beans and gungo peas (especially at Christmas time).

Preparation time: soaking overnight + 15 minutes + about 2½ hours cooking. Serves 6–8

250 g/1 cup dried red peas (red kidney beans or gungo peas), soaked overnight

375 ml/1½ cups coconut milk

400 g/2 cups white rice

3 spring onions

1 fresh thyme sprig

1 scotch bonnet pepper

salt and freshly ground black pepper

1. Drain and rinse the beans. Place the beans in a large, heavy saucepan with a tight fitting lid. Add enough water to cover them. Bring to the boil and boil rapidly for 10 minutes and then reduce the heat and cook for about 2 hours or until tender. Top up the water as necessary.

2. Add the coconut milk, rice, spring onions, thyme, salt and pepper. Add enough water so that there is about 2½ times as much liquid as rice and beans (see Cook's tip).

3. Drop the whole pepper in and bring to the boil. Immediately cover the pot and turn the heat down to its lowest. Allow the rice to steam slowly for about 25–30 minutes. Do not open the pot or stir the rice during this process or it will become sticky. When finished, all the liquid should be absorbed and the rice tender.

4. Remove the pepper, spring onions and the thyme sprig, Fluff the rice and serve warm.

Cook's tip: When steaming rice, it is quite a popular practice to use this trick to measure. Once you have added your rice and it is sitting level in the pot, add liquid (coconut milk and water) until it reaches one finger joint above the rice (about an inch). You can stick a clean finger in and it doesn't seem to matter what quantity of rice you are making it always comes out right. Make sure the pot is large enough as the rice will more than double in size when cooked.

Cornmeal Coo-Coo

Cornmeal (polenta) will be found in every self-respecting storecupboard throughout the islands. We make porridge, dumplings, pone, fritters, pudding, pastelles and coo-coo with it. Cheap, filling and tasty, it's been on the table for many years.

Coo-coo, or turned cornmeal, is thicker than porridge and more often has a little coconut milk and seasonings. It is moulded and cooled until it becomes hard enough to slice. Made bland, with little more than salt and pepper, with okra or onions, or filled with meat or just about anything else it is often sliced and re-fried or baked.

Cornmeal has also had the unfortunate association of being cheap enough to be used as dog food. So when my friends jokingly ask me to bring my 'dog food dish' as the contribution to the pot-luck party, you know a dog's dinner can't be so bad!
Preparation and cooking time: 40 minutes + 30 minutes cooling. Serves 12–18

1 sweet red pepper
1.5 litres/6¼ cups water
3 chicken stock cubes
350 g/2 cups cornmeal
1 tbsp butter
60 ml/¼ cup coconut milk

1 onion, chopped
8 okra, cut into rings or 300 g/10 oz sweetcorn
    kernels stripped from the cob
4 spring onions, chopped (green and white parts)
salt and pepper

1. Preheat the oven to 350°C/180°F/Gas Mark 4. Put the red pepper to roast in the oven. The red pepper's skin will be scorched when it is ready, in about 20 minutes. Put in a plastic bag, knot the end and leave until cool enough to handle.
2. Meanwhile, boil the water in a large pot and add the chicken cubes. Wet the cornmeal thoroughly before adding slowly to the boiling stock. Keep stirring so it won't get lumpy. Add the butter and coconut milk. Keep the heat medium to low, just enough to keep it bubbling.
3. Strip the skin off the pepper, de-seed it, dice the flesh and put half of it in the hot cornmeal and continue to cook, stirring from time to time.
4. After 15 minutes, add the onion and okras. Keep stirring on and off, try not to let the cornmeal stick too much at the bottom of the pot. Cook for 40 minutes.
5. Check the seasoning, adding salt and pepper if necessary and add the spring onions and the other half of the pepper. It should now be quite thick and pulling away from the edges of the pot.
6. Grease either mini cupcake tins, or a fancy metal tin. Use any shape you wish. Sprinkle the reserved red pepper in the bottom of the tin and then pour in the cornmeal.
7. After a few minutes the surface will begin to harden and you will be able to feel when it is firm to touch. When it is cool, turn out and slice. Serve warm, cold or re-heated. It will last, covered, in the refrigerator for a couple of days. Serve with Love Apple (Tomato) Sauce (see page 194).

Cook's tip: Bubbling cornmeal can be very hot, so be very careful not to get burned.

FIERY SAUCES, PICKLES & DRESSINGS

My kitchen is always full of jars of condiments, pickles and sauces. I find it the easiest way to alter the mood of everything from eggs through sandwiches to a main course, simply by adding a drop of something. There's nothing nicer with a jerk sandwich than a dollop of sorrel or mango chutney, or than a drop of pepper sherry in the soup.

Naturally, as pepper-loving people we split hairs over the variety of peppers we have met and the ways we can eat them. It is a taste you develop as a youngster and both tolerance and appreciation tend to grow over time. One can discern many notes of flavour in a pepper and it is not only about heat. Ten peppers from the same field can have different heat quotients and we know this because someone named Scoville developed a technique to measure the units of heat. We usually mean hot peppers when we say 'do you want some pepper?'; bell peppers will be referred to as sweet peppers and black pepper as such.

Habañeros are more popular in the Caribbean than jalapenos or Tabasco peppers and, to be truthful, they tend to be a lot hotter. I can hear my friends in the southern US ready to challenge that statement. Yes, some chillies are quite fierce and we also use bird peppers – those tiny little monsters. The Trinidadians use Congo peppers, and the West Indian red, a relatively new variety, is used for red pepper sauces. The most popular habañero used in Jamaica, though, is the scotch bonnet (which looks like its description); they only come in green or yellow and are cherished for their unique flavour.

I don't know how true this is but it is said that after consuming hot peppers the body secretes endorphins, which are similar to opiates and stimulate the pleasure centres in the brain. Well, I'm always happy when I'm eating pepper.

Creamy Coconut Dressing with Angostura Bitters

This is a delicate dressing with subtle undertones. Serve with a seafood or vegetable salad when you feel in the mood for something gentle.

Preparation time: 10 minutes. Serves: 4–6 (makes about 125 ml/1/2 cup)

70 ml/1/4 cup coconut cream

70 ml/1/4 cup soured cream

6 drops of Angostura bitters

1/4 tsp ground allspice

1 tsp honey

1/2 tsp very finely chopped scotch bonnet pepper

1 tsp white wine vinegar

1. Mix all of the ingredients together. Let sit a while in the refrigerator before serving.

Creamy Lime Sauce

This sauce is ideal for fish or salad.
Makes about 125 ml/1/2 cup

2 tbsp lime juice

1 tsp grated lime zest

1 tbsp snipped fresh chives

1/2 tsp hot pepper sauce

125 ml/1/2 cup soured cream

70 ml/1/4 cup mayonnaise

salt and pepper

1. Mix everything together. Check the balance between salt and lime and adjust to your taste.

Fiery Guava Dipping Sauce or Glaze

Guavas can be found everywhere around the Caribbean but are cherished particularly in the Spanish islands, where guava is used in many forms, from juices to paste.

Preparation and cooking time: 20 minutes roasting + 10 minutes. Serves 6–8 (makes about 225 ml/1 cup)

1 head of garlic

1 tsp olive oil

175 g guava jelly or redcurrant jelly

2 tbsp white wine vinegar

1 tsp hot pepper sauce (optional, for added heat)

1 tsp chopped fresh parsley

1 tsp chopped fresh coriander

1. Preheat the oven to 180°C/350°F/Gas Mark 4. Cut off the top of a whole head of garlic, pour over the olive oil, wrap it in foil and roast for about 15–20 minutes, until soft.
2. Squeeze the cloves out of their skins and crush them in a saucepan. Add all other glaze ingredients (except parsley and coriander). Stir and bring to a simmer, making sure the guava jelly is melted.
3. Cool slightly before serving. Sprinkle on chopped herbs.

Guava Vinaigrette

This is very similar to Fiery Guava Dipping Sauce or Glaze (see above) but in a version suitable for using as a salad dressing.

Preparation and cooking time: 20 minutes roasting + 5 minutes. Serves 4 (makes about 125 ml/½ cup)

3 cloves of roasted garlic (see page 190), crushed

3 tbsp wine vinegar

2 tbsp guava jelly or redcurrant jelly

70 ml/¼ cup olive oil

½ tbsp finely chopped fresh oregano

salt and pepper

1. Squeeze the softened garlic into a bowl and mash with the vinegar.
2. Melt the jelly in a small saucepan and pour into the vinegar mixture.
3. Whisk in the oil slowly, and then whisk in the oregano and salt and pepper.

Cook's tip: If you go ahead and roast a whole head of garlic, reserve the leftover cloves and crush with a stick of soft butter for a nice nutty spread.

Coriander Vinaigrette

This dressing is great for, chicken, seafood or vegetable salads.
Preparation time: 10 minutes. Serves 6–8 (makes about 150 ml/¼ pint)

2 tsp brown sugar

70 ml/¼ cup balsamic vinegar

1 tbsp lemon juice

125 ml/½ cup olive oil

1 garlic clove, pressed

½ tsp hot pepper sauce

125 ml/½ cup finely chopped coriander

salt and pepper

1. In a bowl, mix the sugar and vinegar until the sugar has dissolved.
2. Add the lemon juice and then whisk in the oil slowly, followed by the rest of the ingredients. Adjust the seasoning to taste.

Lime Vinaigrette

This dressing is based on a standard vinaigrette recipe but using lime instead of vinegar. The sharpness of the lime cuts through the oily base and complements any salad containing fruit.
Preparation time: 10 minutes. Serves 4–6 (makes about 125 ml/½ cup)

2 tbsp lime juice

2 tsp sugar

1 tsp Dijon mustard

½ tsp very finely minced or pressed garlic

1 tsp snipped fresh chives

½ tsp grated lime zest

70 ml/¼ cup olive oil

1. Blend the lime juice, sugar, mustard, garlic, chives and lime zest together, using a whisk.
2. Then add the oil slowly, whisking continuously. Toss with the salad just before serving.

Gingery Pickled Beets with Cinnamon & Pepper

Beets are supposed to be very good for you and they are really simple to prepare. Jamaican ginger is legendary for its strength and flavour. Eat the beet pieces on the side with a main course or with other salads.

Preparation time: 15 minutes + 45–60 minutes cooking. Serves 8–10

4 large beetroots

1½ tbsp sugar

1 tsp minced fresh root ginger

125 ml/½ cup cane vinegar or distilled (white) malt vinegar

60 ml/¼ cup water

1 cinnamon stick

½ scotch bonnet pepper, sliced (optional)

1. Boil the beets in a large pan of water until tender, 45–60 minutes.
2. Cool, peel off the skins and slice the beets into wedges. Place in a shallow bowl in one layer.
3. Heat the sugar, ginger, vinegar and water until just boiling and add the cinnamon stick and scotch bonnet, if using. Pour over the sliced beets and allow to sit until cooled.

Cook's tip: Pickled beets can be stored in the refrigerator for up to a month but they will gets hotter the longer you leave the pepper in, so you might want to control that. Try this recipe with baby beets but remember that their cooking time may be a little shorter.

Love Apple (Tomato) Sauce

Tomatoes (also known as 'love apples') grow to a glorious level of sweet ripeness in the Caribbean sunshine. This sauce incorporates Middle-Eastern style in the use of honey to sweeten slightly. I suggest you serve this with Cornmeal Pumpkin Fritters or Cornmeal Coo-Coo (see pages 49 and 185), though you will probably find many other uses. It's quick and fabulous!
Preparation time: 10 minutes. Serves 6–8

1 tbsp butter

6 fat, ripe tomatoes , skinned, de-seeded and chopped

1–2 tbsp honey

salt and white pepper

1. Melt the butter in a little pan and add the tomatoes, honey and salt and pepper.
2. Cook for about 5 minutes until the tomatoes are soft. Serve warm.

Tamarind Tartare

The use of tamarind in this classic sauce adds a completely different dimension to it. Make plenty – you won't be able to stop eating it! It is a fabulous accompaniment to many fish or chicken dishes.
Preparation time: 5 minutes + 1 hour standing. Serves 6–8 (makes about 200 ml/7 fl oz)

150 ml/¼ pint mayonnaise

1 tsp chopped fresh chives or tarragon

1 tsp chopped capers

2 tsp chopped fresh parsley

2 tsp chopped gherkins

1 tbsp tamarind paste

1. Mix all the ingredients together and then set aside to stand for at least one hour before serving, to allow the flavours to mingle.

Cook's tip: Tamarind paste can be bought already prepared without having to soak it first and strain it. If you are unable to find this particular variety use the tamarind block and soak it first and then strain it.

Escoveitch Pickle Sauce

Jamaica

Pickled vegetables are common in many cuisines but in the Caribbean our pickles usually include the omnipresent hot peppers. One might just take a piece of vegetable to have on the side with a meal or a spoonful of the spicy vinegar might be added to a dish. For escoveitch fish, though, you'll use both liquid and pickle pieces to souse your fried fish.

I remember pickle competitions at school fairs, where pieces of carrot and cho-cho (christophene) were cut in shapes to make elaborate scenes inside the jar: 'eyes' made of allspice berries deftly tucked into fish shapes cut out of vegetables, or a colourful flower garden, for instance.

Escoveitch sauce is a more casually thrown together pickle wherein the vegetables are usually julienned like large matchsticks and the onions and peppers cut into rings.

Preparation and cooking time: 15 minutes. Makes a jarful (it will keep for several months)

625 ml/2½ cups cane vinegar or distilled (white) malt vinegar

1 christophene, peeled, cored and julienned

2 carrots, peeled and julienned

1 onion, cut into thin rings

1–3 hot peppers, de-seeded and sliced into rings

2 tbsp allspice berries

3 garlic cloves

a pinch of salt

1. Put the vinegar in a non-reactive saucepan and add all the ingredients. Heat for 5 minutes until the vegetables soften a bit.
2. Store in a large jar with a secure lid and use at your pleasure. Make sure that the vegetables are covered with vinegar; add more if necessary. Or use immediately with fish or chicken; each serving gets a spoonful or two of the flavourful vinegar and as many pieces of pickled vegetables as you like.

Pepper Sherry

Remove the stems from a few whole hot peppers and halve them or prick them with a fork or skewer. Then simply soak in your favourite sherry or rum for a few days and then add a dash of the sherry to soups or stews when cooking. If you succumb to temptation and eat the pepper you can always add another one to the sherry later. This keeps in a well sealed bottle for about six months.

Hot Peppers The hottest part of a pepper is the membrane and seeds and, unless you are quite pepper-mad and want a big surprise in a tiny package, I recommend that you carefully scrape, de-seed your hot peppers and discard the seeds and pith before chopping up the peppers. Please use all precautions, like wearing gloves and remember to wash your hands carefully if you handle hot peppers as they will make you cry a lot more than onions.

If you have overestimated your tolerance, eat something sweet or dairy (like yogurt) to relieve the burning in your mouth. Water will only move the pain around as the heat is carried in the chilli oil so isn't dissolved in water.

Hot peppers are popular in hot climates because they make you sweat and thereby cool you down but it is quite funny really, when you look at it, how pepper-lovers will sweat and cry and still go back for more. Happiness is a hot, hot pepper!

Lime Pepper Jelly

Preparation and cooking time: 30 minutes. Makes 450 g/1 lb

1 green sweet pepper
3 green habañero peppers
juice of 2 limes
225 ml/1 cup cane vinegar or distilled (white) malt vinegar

375 g/1½ cups sugar
2½ tbsp liquid fruit pectin (e.g. Certo)
1 lime sliced thinly, then each slice cut into
6 little wedges

1. Put on your gloves to chop the peppers. Remove stems, membrane and seeds and then chop the sweet pepper and all but one of the hot peppers using a blender or food processor, with a little vinegar.
2. Chop the reserved hot pepper very finely, by hand and set aside.
3. Blend the peppers and vinegar. Strain and add to the sugar and lime juice in a non-reactive pan. Bring to a boil. Reduce the heat and simmer for about 10 minutes.
4. Stir in the pectin and remove from the heat. Allow to cool down and thicken a bit and then stir in the reserved chopped pepper and lime pieces. Mix when setting so lime pieces remain suspended.
5. Allow to cool completely before using. If not using straight away, pour into a sterile jar (a 16-oz Kilner jar is ideal).

Red Pepper Jelly

The ultimate hot and sweet condiment. Use a small amount with any dish instead of hot sauce.
Preparation and cooking time: 30 minutes. Makes 450 g/1 lb

1 red sweet pepper
3 habanero peppers (reserve 1 for chopping, which can be a
different colour for contrast)

225 ml/1 cup cane vinegar or distilled (white) malt vinegar
375 g/1½ cups sugar
2½ tbsp liquid fruit pectin (e.g. Certo)

1. Put on your gloves to chop the peppers. Remove stems, membrane and seeds and then chop the sweet pepper and all but one of the hot peppers using a blender or food processor, with a little vinegar.
2. Chop the reserved hot pepper very finely, by hand and set aside.
3. Blend the peppers and vinegar. Strain and add to the sugar in a non-reactive pan. Bring to a boil. Reduce the heat and simmer for about 10 minutes.
4. Stir in the pectin and remove from heat. Allow to cool down and thicken a bit, then stir in the reserved chopped pepper.

ICY FRUITS, STICKY PUDDINGS & DELICATE DESSERTS

My sister once baked a cake to take to the country for the family weekend. She iced it delicately and sprinkled those colourful 'hundreds and thousands' over the top. There wasn't much appreciation for the modern art which developed on the icing while travelling in the back of a hot car and when we discovered that only the serrated bread knife could cut into it, she was laughed to derision by our teenage cousins. To my knowledge, she has never baked since.

I tell you this because many people are intimidated by cooking and even one failure can destroy a potential lifetime of pleasure in the kitchen. Even the best cooks make flops occasionally. I think one has to cook first for oneself, and the simpler the better. Don't take on a major operation when all you want is something tasty to eat. Think of the number of meals we eat in a lifetime. So what if a few get scorched, over salted, or over sweetened (some will say there is no such thing)? Don't give up. Choose the easiest dishes first and confidence will grow. I find desserts the hardest.

Most of us crave something sweet at the end of a meal, even if just a taste. Some of you, and you know who you are, even need to know what's for dessert before the main meal starts so you can judge how much space to leave.

We have such a huge variety of seasonal fruits in the Caribbean we are never short of a treat and these are often the basis of our sweets. Matrimony is the union of grapefruit and star apple, a dark, round fruit the size of an orange with a milky, purplish pulp. When you cut it crosswise the seeds form a star pattern. Pineapples are indigenous and mangoes (brought from India) grow in many varieties everywhere. I remember how we used to sit in the classroom at school during mango season and be thoroughly distracted by the blackie mangoes (small, green, extremely sweet and hairy) turning yellow on the trees outside. The only calculations going on in our math class were how high is that bunch and how fast can I reach it after the bell goes?

Some of us kept huge stashes in our desks and would dare a pretence of looking for something while having a quick bite, then emerging with hairy teeth and a yellow moustache. Guinep season in this respect, was probably worse. Guineps are a popular, small, round fruit which grows in clusters like green grapes. Hard-skinned, the fleshy stone is popped in your mouth and they are sucked one at a time. The large trees grow wild all over the region.

Many of the more complex desserts are traditional and many of them can be traced to their European roots. Christmas pudding and dark fruit cakes, for instance, are quite widespread, particularly in the English-influenced islands, and there is a ritual to getting the fruit soaking on time. It was quite the topic of November telephone calls, to make sure all my mother's sisters had found the necessary amounts of citron, raisins and cherries. They might have competed amongst themselves, but only 'Gaga's' (my grandmother) was held in the place of honour.

The popular 'essence' that is used in puddings and fruit cakes is a blend of almond extract, vanilla and rose-water. The addition of rum, Angostura bitters, and local liqueurs have perked up our desserts and puddings for many years.

Many sweets are flavoured with coconut. Both canned evaporated milk and condensed milk are traditional staples used for dessert-making from a time when storage of cream was impractical. They also form the basis of the ever-popular 'flans', which are abundant. There are many good pâtisseries, especially on the French islands, and the best hotels have wonderful chocolate and pastry chefs who satisfy the big sweet tooth which we are always trying to thrill.

Just remember, as Miss Piggy says: 'don't eat anything you can't lift'!

Minty Pineapple Mojito

The pineapple is on the Jamaican Coat of Arms – a symbol of friendship and hospitality. This indigenous fruit was introduced to Columbus by the native Indians on his 'discovery' visit to the islands and represented the height of gastronomic celebration as it was slowly introduced to European and American society.

The pineapple was taken to Hawaii years ago, where it developed into a huge industry. The shapes and sizes vary considerably throughout the Caribbean and you will find the tall conical ones in Guadeloupe quite different to the large round ones in Puerto Rico. There is nothing to compare with a cold, freshly peeled, sweet, juicy 'sugar loaf' pineapple. The skins are soaked in water for a day or two and strained off to make a drink.

This recipe was influenced by Jamie Oliver's version. It captures huge enjoyment in its simplicity.

Preparation time: 15 minutes + 30 minutes chilling. Serves 4–6

1 large pineapple, peeled, cored and cut in 5-cm/2-inch chunks
70 ml/¼ cup Wray & Nephew Overproof Rum (optional)
75 g/¼ cup granulated sugar
1 bunch of fresh mint, picked (½ cup mint leaves)

1.   Place the pineapple chunks in a glass bowl with the rum and chill for half an hour.
2.   Using a mortar and pestle, crush the mint with the sugar (it will bruise the leaves). Do this until the leaves are well mashed up.
3.   Just before serving, remove the pineapple and drain off any excess juice. Toss with the minty sugar and serve immediately to retain the crunchy texture of the sugar. The fruit will disappear before you can blink!

Tropical Fruit Salad & Ice Cream with Hot Citrus Syrup

It may sound slightly odd to have hot pepper with a fruit dessert; the taste is a little startling, and your cheeks might pucker slightly, but it is very enjoyable. Leave it out if you prefer. Either buy some vanilla ice cream to serve with it or make your own.

Preparation and cooking time: 20 minutes. Serves 4

½ small pineapple, peeled and cored

1 mango, peeled and stoned

2 bananas, peeled and tossed in lime juice over to prevent discoloration

1 small papaya, peeled and de-seeded

½ medium-size watermelon, peeled and de-seeded (about 450 g/1 lb)

vanilla ice cream, to serve

fresh mint sprigs, to garnish

For the hot citrus syrup:

juice of 2 oranges,

juice of 1 lime

125 g/½ cup soft brown sugar

1 tbsp dark rum

½ tsp very finely chopped hot pepper, e.g. scotch bonnet (optional)

grated orange and lime zest

1. Cut all the fruit into 2.5-cm/1-inch cubes (or thereabouts) place in a bowl and mix gently.
2. Strain the orange and lime juices (you should have about 225 ml/1 cup in total).
3. Add all the hot citrus syrup ingredients to a non-stick pan, with the exception of the zest. Stir and heat until it reduces a little, about 5–10 minutes.
4. Place a serving of fruit salad and a scoop of vanilla ice cream on each plate and pour over the warm sauce. Sprinkle with the zest and add a sprig of mint to each plate before serving.

Cook's tip: Choose your fruit, mix or match. Make an ice bowl with flowers or leaves frozen in it to present the fruit salad, if not serving the syrup.

Grapefruit & Angostura Bitters Sorbet

The abundance of exotic fruit and the hot climate of the Caribbean just call for refreshing fruit sorbets. For a really smooth sorbet you should have an ice-cream or sorbet machine; however I think it tastes just as good and is as equally refreshing when the sorbet is made by hand and has more of a 'water ice' consistency.
Preparation time: 30 minutes + 6 hours freezing. Makes approximately 1.5 litres/2½ pints

For the basic sugar syrup (makes 400 ml/14 fl oz):
250 g/9 oz caster sugar
400 ml/14 fl oz water

For the sorbet:
juice of 4 ripe pink grapefruit
juice of 2 large oranges
Angostura bitters
juice of 1 lime

1. First of all make a basic sugar syrup by dissolving the sugar in the water in a heavy-based saucepan over low heat. Increase the heat to high and boil for a couple of minutes. Remove from the heat and set aside to cool and then chill in the fridge for an hour.
2. Mix the fruit juice and chilled syrup together and then stir in a few dashes of the Angostura bitters and lime juice.
3. Freeze in a shallow container for three to four hours, beating with an electric or hand whisk two or three times during freezing. Or, if you have an ice cream machine, churn until almost firm and then freeze in a plastic container.
4. Serve in scoops or shavings.

Watermelon Sorbet You will need 2–2½ kg/4½–5½ lb to make 500 ml/18 fl oz of juice. To make the juice, skin, de-seed and chop up the fruit, pulverise in a blender and then pass through a sieve. Add 400 ml/14 fl oz of sugar syrup and then freeze, following the directions above. Serve with shredded mint leaves.

Pomegranate & Rose-water Sorbet You will need 8 pomegranates, to make 500 ml/18 fl oz of juice. To make the juice, cut the pomegranates in quarters and remove all the fruit, being careful to avoid the yellow membranes, which are bitter. Place the fruit in a blender and liquidise. Then pass the mixture through a sieve to remove all the seeds. Add 400 ml/14 fl oz of sugar syrup, 1 tbsp of rose-water and the juice of 1 lime. Then freeze, following the directions above.

Mango Sorbet You will need approximately 4 large juicy mangoes, to make 500 ml/18 fl oz of pulp. To make the juice, peel and cut the mango flesh into chunks and blend in a liquidiser. Alternatively, use canned mango pulp. Add 400 ml/14 fl oz of sugar syrup and the juice of 1 lime and then freeze, following the directions above.

Blue Mountain Coffee Flan

If you love desserts, you'll certainly adore this one. The combination of the subtle flavour of the Blue Mountain coffee and the satiny texture of the creamy flan work brilliantly together.
Preparation time: 1 hour + 45 minutes cooking + 2 hours cooling. Serves 8

225 g/8 oz caster sugar
6 eggs
2 egg yolks
600 ml/1 pint double cream
1 tsp vanilla essence
125 ml/¼ cup very strong, black Jamaican Blue Mountain Coffee™

1. Preheat the oven to 180°C/350°F/Gas Mark 4.
2. Make the caramel syrup: heat half of the sugar in a heavy-bottomed pan over low heat for about 5–10 minutes, until the sugar has melted and has turned golden brown. Keep tipping the pan, taking care not to let the sugar burn as it is melting.
3. Pour the syrup into the bottom of a 20 cm/8 in flan dish. Set aside while you make the custard.
4. Combine the eggs, yolks, cream, vanilla and remaining sugar in a medium-size saucepan. Turn the heat to low and gently cook the mixture, stirring constantly, until it is thick enough to coat the back of the spoon.
5. Remove from the heat and stir in the coffee.
6. Pour into the flan dish. Set the dish into a baking dish and pour in enough warm water to come halfway up the sides of the flan dish. Then place the baking dish in the centre of the oven. Cook for 45 minutes, or until the custard has set firmly.
7. Carefully remove from the oven and set aside to cool. When cool, place a serving dish on top, invert and turn the flan out of the flan dish. Leave to cool for a couple of hours before serving.

Real Vanilla & other Caribbean Ice Creams

Rich and creamy, this is the ultimate in vanilla ice cream. Definitely not suitable for weight-watchers … made for hedonists only!
Preparation and cooking time 20 minutes + 1 hour cooling + freezing overnight. Makes 750 ml/1¼ pints

225 ml/1 cup whole milk
600 ml/1 pint double cream
1 vanilla pod, split

6 egg yolks
225 g/8 oz caster sugar

1.   Put the milk and cream in a saucepan, scrape in the vanilla seeds and add the pod and heat very gently until hot (or until bubbles start to form around the edge). Do not allow to boil though. Remove from the heat and set aside to cool a little.

2.   Whisk the egg yolks and sugar together in a bowl until thick and pale. Slowly pour the cream mixture into the beaten egg yolks, whisking continuously.

3.   Return the mixture to the saucepan and cook over low heat, stirring constantly with a wooden spoon, for at least 15 minutes, or until it is thick enough to coat the back of the spoon. Do not overcook the custard or it will curdle. Remove from the heat and set aside to cool for about an hour.

4.   Remove the vanilla pod (or strain to remove both pod and seeds if you prefer). Pour the cooled mixture into an ice-cream maker and freeze until just firm, following the manufacturer's instructions.

5.   Alternatively, if you do not have an ice-cream maker, you should pour your cooled custard into a metal bowl and place in the freezer for 2½ hours or until it starts to freeze around the edges. Beat the mixture with an electric hand mixer for a few minutes and then return to the freezer for 3–4 hours or overnight.

Coconut Ice Cream Substitute 450 ml/16 fl oz of single cream and 200 ml/7 fl oz of thick coconut milk for the double cream.

Coffee Ice Cream Substitute 225 ml/8 fl oz of double-strength Jamaica Blue Mountain Coffee™ for the milk. If you would like a little texture, add about 1 tbsp of the coffee granules as well.

Ginger Ice Cream Add 175 g/6 oz of finely chopped stem ginger to the Real Vanilla Ice Cream mix before freezing.

Grape Nut Ice Cream Add 110 g/4 oz of grape nuts to the Real Vanilla Ice Cream mix before freezing.

Cook's tip: There is nothing nicer for a simple dessert than adding a few dashes of Angostura bitters to plain vanilla ice cream. Then top with a handful of toasted slivered almonds.

Mango Tart

This delicious tart is deceptively easy to make. However, you will need a frying pan with a steel handle rather than plastic, so it can be put in the oven. I have used frozen puff pastry here, which makes an excellent substitute for home-made puff pastry and speeds up the preparation process considerably.

Preparation time: 15 minutes + 25 minutes cooking. Serves 6

4 mangoes, peeled and sliced
60 g/2 oz unsalted butter
150 g/5 oz caster sugar
225 g/8 oz frozen puff pastry, defrosted
flour for rolling out

1.   Place the mango slices in a colander to drain for 30 minutes.
2.   Preheat the oven to 200°C/400°F/Gas Mark 6.
3.   Melt the butter in a 20 cm/8-inch frying pan. Add the sugar and allow to melt slowly, without stirring, over medium heat. Tip the pan frequently to help the sugar to melt.
4.   When the sugar has turned golden, add the mango slices and turn up the heat. The mangoes will let out a lot of liquid so cook for 10–15 minutes, stirring frequently, until the liquid has evaporated and the sauce is thick and caramelly. Remove from the heat.
5.   Meanwhile, roll out the puff pastry large enough to more than cover the mango. Pack down the mango and then cover with pastry, pushing down the sides. Make a hole in the centre.
6.   Place in the centre of the oven to cook the pastry for about 20–25 minutes.
7.   Remove from the oven, leave for a couple of minutes, and then turn out on to a plate and serve with vanilla ice cream.

Cook's tip: If the pastry starts to brown too much before it is cooked, cover it with some foil.

Little Rum & Chocolate Puddings

These little puddings make a spectacular dessert for a dinner party. The only hassle is that you have to cook them just before you serve them and the timing is essential, but one mouthful makes it all worthwhile.

Preparation and cooking time: 15 minutes + chilling overnight + 15 minutes cooking. Serves 6

5 eggs, plus 5 egg yolks

125 g/4½ oz caster sugar

225 g/8 oz unsalted butter, plus a little bit more for greasing the moulds

225 g/8 oz dark chocolate (70% cocoa solids), broken up

4 tablespoons rum

100 g/3½ oz plain flour

icing sugar, to decorate

1. The day before you wish to serve the puddings, make up the mixture: beat the eggs, egg yolks and sugar together until the mixture is pale yellow.
2. Melt the chocolate and butter slowly together in a heatproof bowl, set over a pan half-filled with hot water.
3. When the mixture has melted, remove from the heat, add the rum and then slowly add the egg mixture, beating constantly. Then fold in the flour.
4. Pour into 180 ml/6 fl oz greased moulds, cover with cling film and chill in the fridge overnight.
5. The following day, preheat the oven to 180°C/350°F/Gas Mark 4. Place in the centre of the oven on a baking sheet and bake for approximately 10–15 minutes, or until the centres puff up and look dry. You will need to check this quite regularly.
6. Turn out on to individual plates, sift over the icing sugar and serve at once.

Soursop Crème with Stewed Guavas

Thanks to Alex Kerr-Wilson's love of soursop, we managed to put this heavenly sweet together in London. Soursop or guanabana is a large prickly green fruit with pulpy white flesh and black seeds. It is too sour to be eaten plain and the pulp is very chewy so squeezing it through a sieve is the way to collect the thick juice, which can then be sweetened and used for flavouring drinks, ice cream or dessert, such as this one.

Canned soursop pulp (found in Asian shops) is an option and works fine for this recipe when fresh soursop is out of season. Outside of the Caribbean, the sweetened juice is sold commercially. (Canned stewed guavas are acceptable.)
Preparation time: 30 minutes + 3 hours chilling. Serves 8–10

225 ml/1 cup soursop purée (1 fresh soursop or use a can)
600 ml/1 pint cream
¾ cup sugar
600 ml/1 pint Greek-style yogurt (or soured cream will do)
juice and grated zest of 1 lime (no pith)
2 tsp vanilla essence
6 tsp gelatine

For the stewed guavas:
4 small guavas
60 ml/¼ cup water
1 tbsp sugar
125 ml/½ cup guava jelly (redcurrant jelly is a good alternative)
zest of I lime, peeled in strips, or fresh mint sprigs, to garnish

1. Remove the pulp from the soursops. Place the pulp in a strainer over a bowl. Using a wooden spoon or spatula, press back and forth until you have gathered as much of the thick purée as you need. Discard the seeds and pulp.
2. Heat the cream and sugar with the lime zest and vanilla. Simmer for a few minutes. Remove from heat and strain to discard the lime zest.
3. Dissolve the gelatine in the lime juice and stir into the hot cream. Whisk in the yogurt and soursop purée until evenly combined.
4. Transfer the mixture into a 2-litre/3½ pint container or ramekins. Chill for about 5 hours or until set.
5. When firm, loosen the edges by carefully the dipping mould partially into hot water and allowing sides to melt just slightly. Unmould.
6. Peel the fresh guavas and cut in half. Scoop out the seeds and cut into bite-size wedges.
7. Stew the guavas slowly in a saucepan with ¼ cup water and a tablespoon of sugar for 5–10 minutes. As soon as they are soft, add the guava or redcurrant jelly and heat to liquefy. If using canned guavas, they will already be stewed in syrup so just drain, remove the seeds and slice. Heat the jelly until it is liquid and then add the guavas.
8. Serve the sauce and guavas warm beside the cold soursop crème(s). Decorate with lime zest or mint leaves.

Cook's tip: These crèmes can be made a few days ahead and kept refrigerated.

drinks

The Caribbean is probably best known for its rum. The distilleries developed alongside the sugar plantations as rum is distilled from molasses. The strong association goes back to days of the Pirates and Buccaneers and Treasure Island's 'Yo ho ho and a bottle of rum!'. Barbados has seen over 350 years of production. Rum is growing once again in popularity and the master blenders are offering some intense and appealing choices. There are deep differences between Jamaican rums like Appleton, Haitian Barbancourt, Trinidadian Angostura, Puerto Rican Don Q and Barbados' Mount Gay; and let's not forget that Bacardi, which originated in Cuba, is now produced in Puerto Rico.

Rum is one of those drinks that the purists don't like messed around and for the well-aged, mellow rums of over ten years vintage, aged in oak caskets (as fine as any cognac), try not to be seen adding cola, coconut water or maraschino cherries and paper umbrellas. It is the younger rums which are used for rum punch, daquiris, mohitos and pina coladas. For cooking, the dark rums are best.

You will have to go to a rum bar to find the really least refined ones and be warned that all white rums are not equal: in Jamaica we have Wray and Nephew's White 12G Overproof and it is hugely popular (great for rum punch). As children, our mothers and grandmas would dab overproof rum all over our bodies to bring a high fever down. With such rapid evaporation, it really works. You could always find some 'Whites' (as we call it) in the medicine cabinet.

Some world-class liqueurs come from this region and you will recognise brands like Tia Maria, and Curaçao, which appear on any well stocked bar. Exotic ingredients like sour orange peel are grown for other large-scale producers.

The Caribbean also boasts internationally recognized beers such as Red Stripe and Carib. And we are probably not far from the Irish in our consumption of stout both Guinness and Dragon.

Coffee, Tea and Cocoa Hot drinks are a traditional start to our day.

Tea might mean any of several infusions: there is 'bush tea' (any infusion of made with boiling water and medicinal herbs), 'green tea' (made with proper tea leaves), 'cocoa tea' (hot chocolate) and 'coffee tea' (coffee). You might need to be specific.

Coffee has been grown commercially in the Caribbean since the eighteenth century, starting in Martinique. The most popular coffee producers are Jamaica, Cuba, Dominican Republic and Puerto Rico. Though coffee is grown elsewhere, these are the best quality. Jamaica Blue Mountain Coffee ™ is recognized as one of the finest in the world and much of the crop is now sold at a premium price, in Japan.

On Spanish islands coffee is enjoyed as 'café con leche', which is made with steaming milk, for breakfast, or as a 'café Cubano', which is a small cup loaded with sugar more like an espresso. In Jamaica many people enjoy theirs with condensed milk or even coconut milk and it is surprising how much instant coffee is used in the region as people bypass great taste for convenience. Coffee is used to flavour ice cream and desserts.

Cocoa has been grown in the region for many years, but production has fallen victim to global pricing. The Cacao plant was discovered in Jamaica by Lord Sloane in 1687 when he was cataloguing plant cuttings. He later developed and owned the patent for what is known today as milk chocolate. Cocoa is both popular and available as a drink and a baking ingredient.

Concoctions There are also a whole range of popular 'health drinks', like beetroot juice, sea moss and concoctions made from various roots. Don't let the 'healthy roots' thing fool you as they can be quite potent. One of the funniest things about the local drinks and home-made versions can be the names: 'sex on the beach', 'dirty banana', 'granny cratch cratch', 'young gal temper', 'staggaback', 'front end lifter' and so they go on with claims galore.

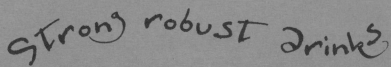
strong robust drinks

Mojito *Serves 1*

fresh mint sprig
½ lime, cut in two
2 tsp caster sugar
ice cubes
club soda (soda water)
50 ml/scant ¼ cup Havana Club Rum

1. Put the first three ingredients into a highball glass and mash together with a spoon. Add ice, soda and rum, stir again thoroughly.

Poncha Crema *Serves 12*

2 eggs, beaten
grated zest of ½ lime
1 can of condensed milk
180 ml/¾ cup evaporated milk
350 ml/1½ cups Angostura Rum
1 cup crushed ice
a dash of Angostura bitters
grated nutmeg

1. Put the egg, lime zest, condensed and evaporated milk in a blender and whiz for about 30 seconds.
2. Share the ice between small glasses and pour the mixture over.
3. Sprinkle with bitters and a grating of nutmeg to taste.

Cuba Libre *Serves 1*

50 ml/scant ¼ cup Havana Club Rum
cola
ice
lime wedge, to decorate

1. Pour the rum over ice in a tall glass. Fill with cola. Decorate with a lime wedge.

Frozen Daiquiri *Serves 1*

50 ml/scant ¼ cup Bacardi White Rum
25 ml/⅛ cup lime juice
1 tsp caster sugar
cracked ice

1. Put the rum, lime juice and sugar in a blender, add the cracked ice and blend until thick. Serve in a cocktail or wide champagne glass.

Pina Colada

50 ml/scant ¼ cup Don Q rum
25 ml/⅛ cup cream of coconut
25 ml/⅛ cup cream
60 ml/¼ cup pineapple juice
crushed ice
unpeeled pineapple slice, to decorate

1. Blend all the ingredients with the ice and pour into a tall goblet. Decorate with a slice of pineapple.

Blue Lagoon *Serves 1*

30 ml/⅛ cup Blue Curacao

30 ml/⅛ cup vodka

ice cubes

lemonade

maraschino cherry

1. Pour the Curacao and vodka over ice in a tall glass, fill with lemonade and drop in a cherry.

Blue Velvet *Serves 1*

60 ml/¼ cup Tia Maria coffee liqueur

60 ml/¼ cup coconut milk

30 ml/⅛ cup double cream

60 ml/¼ cup strong Jamaica Blue Mountain Coffee™

ice cubes

3 coffee beans, to decorate

1. Pour the ingredients over ice in an old-fashioned glass, and mix. Float the coffee beans on top.

Rum Punch *Serves 2*

Follow this rhyme and you'll never forget the proportions: '1 of sour, 2 of sweet, 3 of strong and 4 of weak'!

30 ml/⅛ cup fresh lime juice

60 ml/¼ cup sugar syrup or 60 g/2 oz sugar

90 ml/⅜ cup Wray and Nephew White Overproof Rum

125 ml/½ cup orange or other fresh fruit juice

2 dashes Angostura Bitters

ice cubes

lime slices

maraschino cherries

1. Mix all the ingredients together and serve with ice in tall tumblers, decorated with a slice of lime and a maraschino cherry. Here's where you can go to town on your décor, even bringing in the paper umbrellas.

Ti Punch *Serves 1*

½ lime

1 tsp granulated sugar

50 ml/scant ¼ cup rum

1. Mix the lime and sugar in a small glass and add the rum.

soft, gentle, quiet drinks

I could not begin to give you recipes for all the wonderful fresh juices and rootsy concoctions you can find in the Caribbean. These are just a few of my favourite ones.

Carrot Juice with Lime *Serves 4–6*

650 g/1½ lb carrots, juiced (about 8 carrots)

1 cm/½-inch piece of fresh root ginger

675–900 ml/3–4 cups water

3–4 limes

about 125 g/½ cup sugar

1. Juice the carrots and ginger whole if using a juicer or peel and cut them up and blend together in a blender or food processor.
2. Add water, lime juice and sugar to taste.
3. Strain, if you have used a blender/processor. Chill before serving.

Soursop Juice *Serves 4*

650–900 g/1½–2 lb ripe soursop

450 ml/¾ pint water

2–4 tbsp condensed milk

a pinch of grated nutmeg

¼ tsp vanilla essence

1. Peel the soursop and place the pulp in a sieve. Push with a wooden spoon until you have extracted as much thick juice as you can. Use about 2 cups of water to get the last juice through and to dilute it slightly. Discard the seeds and pulp.
2. Add about 2 tbsp of condensed milk and taste. You can dilute it more or make it sweeter if you wish. Add the nutmeg and vanilla. Serve chilled.

Lime Squash *Serves 1*

45 ml/3 tbsp fresh lime juice

1–2 tbsp sugar syrup or sugar

1 glass of club soda (soda water)

ice cubes, to serve

maraschino cherry (optional), to decorate

1. Pour the lime juice into a glass and add syrup to sweeten to taste. Add the soda water and pour over ice in a tall glass. A maraschino cherry is the popular decoration.

Sorrel & Ginger *Serves 8–10*

Usually served at Christmas time, sorrel is bright red drink made from the sepals of the sorrel plant. It has a very refreshing quality and can be served with or without the rum.

25 g/1 oz dried sorrel

7.5 cm/3-inch cinnamon stick

1 orange

6 cloves

1 tbsp peeled and chopped fresh root ginger

450 g/1 lb sugar

1.75 litres/3 pints boiling water.

6 tbsp Appleton Rum (optional)

cracked ice, to serve

1. Remove the zest from the orange with a zester or peel it off carefully and cut into shreds with a knife.
2. In a large, non-reactive container, put all the ingredients except the boiling water and rum.
3. Pour the boiling water over, cover and allow to steep overnight.
4. Strain and add rum, if using, adjusting the strength to your liking.
5. Present in a punch bowl or glass jug. Pour over cracked ice to serve.

parties
& MENU PLANNING

Delicious food is enhanced by atmosphere. I don't mind how simple or rustic, or how grand and formal, but alfresco dining, with laughter, is my ultimate delight.

Not so long ago, in Guadaloupe, I had one of the most magical meals, with new friends. It was under a tin-covered shed in the middle of a cane field. On arrival we fixed ourselves 'ti-punch' (rum, sugar and lime) from the open bar. This is a little pre-meal ritual which took very little getting used to. We ordered many dishes. I had met Marie-France on the plane coming over and she could not have been more generous, even to the point of lending a stranger like me her sister's phone. Caribbean people can be like that.

She called her friends and they kept arriving. We shared bites of tasty 'morue à l'oignon' (salt fish and rice with onions), lentil stew, delicious 'court bouillon de poisson' (whole red snapper in a tomato-based sauce, see page 97), which is a classic Guadeloupian dish. There was a tasty 'ragout de coq' (free-range rooster), whose doomed companions were still running around the yard nearby. On the table was bread, wine, lime wedges and the most ferocious habañero pepper I have ever eaten: 'bonda a mon jak' is the French Creole description, which refers to a Mrs Jack, who is a very hot lady!

The sky went dark but we were all in a fun mood and the silliness and laughter never stopped. The rain fell, we moved our chairs for more shelter, took pictures, drank some wine and continued the hilarity through the fresh-peeled oranges and delicious cups of espresso. It was not until everyone had gone back to work that I realised it was just a regular Wednesday afternoon in Guadeloupe.

Once you have pulled together the right group and set the best atmosphere you can, the food almost becomes secondary. Having said that, the food you choose should be appropriate for both the occasion and your guests.

And remember, there is music for every Caribbean occasion! Choose from a selection of reggae, calypso, zouk, soca, salsa, dancehall, mento, ska, rocksteady, local jazz and 'lover's rock': take your pick and pump up the party!

Caribbean Brunch Party This menu works for christenings, small weddings or occasions when children and family and friends of all ages need to mingle. Starting late on a Saturday or Sunday morning, no one has had much breakfast and it goes on past lunchtime. Bring it out in courses. Yellow and orange tones for your table setting and flowers are delightful for this time of day.

Tropical Fruit Salad & Ice Cream with Hot Citrus Syrup
(no hot pepper) (page 202)
Sorrel & Ginger (page 223)

~

Hard dough toast with marmalade and guava jelly
Bul Jol (page 47) and Coconut Bake (page 177)

~

Jamaica Blue Mountain Coffee™

~

Lightly Curried Ackee
Fried or Roast Breadfruit slices (page 48)
Cornmeal Coo Coos (page 185) or Mini Tortillas (page 178)
Avocado slices with Lime Vinaigrette (page 191)

~

Banana Fritters
Ice Cream (page 207)

~

Ginger Beer and Soursop Juice (page 223)
Red Stripe Beer

Caribbean Picnic I suppose a sunny, summer Sunday is the traditional day for a picnic. Luckily, we have many choice days in the Caribbean and the venue can be anywhere from the beach, a river "lime", country cricket match or hiking in the hills. Be sure to pack enough large throws and a few cushions so everyone can stretch out and do what comes naturally after the meal. Don't forget the corkscrew or the bottle opener. Fresh, cool water will always be appreciated. (If you are going somewhere where you can cook or barbecue, bring your chicken already cut up and marinated.)

Mini Tortillas (page 178) or Cornmeal Coo-Coos (page 185) or
Green Banana and Salt Fish Salad (page 76)

~

Cold Grilled Jerk Chicken (page 130) or
Five-spice Roast Chicken (page 110)

~

Escoveitched Fish (page 91)

~

Prepared fresh fruit, such as watermelon or pineapple

~

A cooler with ice, ginger beer, Ting (a grapefruit juice soft drink),
water, iced or hot coffee

Sunday Lunch for Six In the Caribbean, it is traditional to have a long lunch on Sunday and it is usually with the family, so it's likely you'll have company in the kitchen. For some reason it is always running a little late … so, while the aperitifs fuel the chatter, start with the Gundy and move on to the next course proper when you're ready.

Solomon Gundy (page 45) and crackers

Caribbean Fish Tea (page 63)

~

Five-spice Roast Chicken (page 110) with roast potatoes and gravy

Rice & Peas (page 183)

Baked Aubergine with Callaloo Rundown (page 167)

Baked Ripe Plantain (page 171)

Fancy Coleslaw (page 75)

~

Blue Mountain Coffee Flan (page 206)

Elegant Caribbean Dinner Imagine a fairly intimate atmosphere, as six people aren't too many. Set lots of candles at different levels, with tropical flowers and real linen napkins in outrageous colours like bougainvillea pink, lime green, papaya and turquoise. If you can lay your hands on a bunch of fresh green bananas and their big leaves, set them diagonally across the table, you'll be ahead of the decorating game. Ban all overhead lighting tonight, except in the kitchen.

Pumpkin Lobster Bisque (page 65) and

Hot Pepper Bread (page 175)

~

Christophene & Cantaloupe Salad (page 75)

~

Jerked Lamb with Guava Glaze (page 131)

Creamed Cassava with Roasted Garlic (page 180) and

Grilled Courgettes

~

Little Rum and Chocolate Puddings (page 211) and Real Vanilla Ice

Cream (page 207) with toasted flaked almonds

and a dash of Angostura bitters

~

Jamaica Blue Mountain Coffee™ and Tia Maria

glossary pictures

1. Coffee
2. Guava
3. Rum
4. June plum
5. Cornmeal
6. Allspice berries
   (pimentos)
7. Plantains
8. Red peppercorns
9. Passion-fruit
10. Mango
11. Breadfruit
12. Gungo peas
13. Christophene
14. White
    peppercorns
15. Star fruit/
    carambola

FRUIT

Banana Both yellow and green bananas are used a great deal in West Indian cooking: yellow ones are used for desserts and breads and the green ones are generally boiled and served as a starchy vegetable (also called ground provisions). In some islands they are referred to as 'figs', which may have originated from the apocryphal story of Adam and Eve using banana leaves rather than fig leaves to cover their nakedness.

Bitter/Valencia/Seville and sour oranges Originally from Spain, the flesh of the sour orange is too sour to eat but is used to make marmalade. Other oranges are used for juice or for drinks such as Curaçao's famous orange liqueur.

Guanabana/soursop A green spiny-skinned fruit. The juicy white flesh consists of numerous segments, mostly seedless (seeds should be avoided). Its flavour is reminiscent of a slightly fermented pineapple and most often used for refreshing drinks and ice creams or sorbets.

Guava A round fruit with a thin yellow skin. The flesh is either white or pink with hard seeds. Eaten as a dessert fruit, stewed, made into jams, jellies and guava paste.

Lime Brought to the islands by early European settlers, lime trees flourished throughout the islands and, together with hot pepper, lime has become one of the most important ingredients of Caribbean cooking. Lime juice is used in most dishes, to clean and season fish, poultry and meat and as a flavouring for a host of vegetable dishes as well as desserts and drinks.

Mango There are hundreds of different varieties of mango in the Caribbean. They range in size from plum-sized to some that weigh more than 1kg (2 or 3 lb). Smooth-skinned, these fruit can vary in colour from green through to yellow, pink and bright red. Mango is generally eaten raw, when ripe, as a dessert or the pulp is puréed and sieved and then made into a refreshing drink. It can also be stewed, made into chutneys and pickles when unripe. Some of the most popular varieties are: Pa Ouis, Julie, East Indian, Bombay, Sugar and Alphonso.

Noni The noni is an evergreen tree whose fruit has a very pungent taste and smell. It is thought to have medicinal properties, and is used in herbal drinks.

Papaya The papaya is a delicious fruit, usually consumed at breakfast with a flavour greatly enhanced by a squeeze of lime juice. They vary in size and a smaller variety was developed for export from the Caribbean for overseas demand. Papaya contains an enzyme that is also used as a meat tenderiser.

Passion-fruit This strongly perfume-flavoured fruit becomes wrinkled as it ripens. The orange pulp inside contains loads of tiny black seeds, which are edible, but most people prefer not to eat them. The pulp is generally strained and diluted into juice or used for flavouring a dish much in the same way as vanilla or a strong alcohol. It is also used for ice creams and sorbets, confectionery and sherbets. To make a litre of juice takes over one hundred fruit!

Pomelo/shaddock Originally from Polynesian this fruit was brought to Jamaica in the 17th century by a British ship captain named Shaddock. The fruit took well to the new soil and before long it spawned a new fruit that had a thinner, yellower skin, which became known as grapefruit.

Sorrel Nothing to do with the British herb of the same name, sorrel is a flower whose fleshy deep red sepal is used to make drinks, jams, jellies, chutney and sauces. Also known as rosella and flor de Jamaica, it is a small red plant belonging to the hibiscus family. The sepals are picked and soaked in water and blended with other flavourings such as ginger. Formerly only available at Christmas time, nowadays it is sold dried and in syrup form as well as fresh, so is available all year round.

Tamarind A sticky brown fruit in a crisp pod, ripe, tart tamarind flesh is used for juice or as a flavouring for both sweet and savoury sauces, as an acidifying agent, as well as for ice cream and drinks. It is available fresh still in the pod, as a compressed block of pulp with the black seeds still in, as a paste and as a concentrate, already diluted with water and seedless.

Ugli This unattractive, lumpy, thick-skinned hybrid citrus fruit earned its name from its appearance. It's a combination of a grapefruit, orange and tangerine with a delicate and slightly tart flavour; like the grapefruit, ugli was developed in Jamaica.

VEGETABLES

Ackee The fruit of a West African tree brought to Jamaica in the 18th century by Captain Bligh. When ripe, the pear-shaped scarlet pod bursts open, exposing the edible cream-coloured aril. Visually, it has been compared to scrambled eggs but there the similarity ends. It is hugely popular in Jamaica although it grows on other islands as well. Available fresh in the islands and exported in cans.

Avocado Caribbean avacado varieties tend to be large and are used mainly for salads and dips.

Breadfruit Originally from the Pacific (remember *Mutiny on the Bounty?*), this large round fruit looks like a green cannonball with a distinctive pattern on the skin. Usually served as a vegetable, boiled, roasted or fried like chips, it is often simply roasted whole in the fire and then cut open and eaten with butter. Its flesh has a bland, starchy flavour and is rich in carbohydrates and vitamins A, B and C. It has a delicious nutty flavour and is sometime used in breads, pies and puddings. It is generally cooked before it is ripe as it tends to become too sickly sweet.

Callaloo Callaloo has become almost a generic name for the leaves of a variety of plants such as taro (dasheen), tannia (malanga) and amaranth (prickly callaloo), which are used mostly for making a soup of the same name. Callalloo soup includes numerous other ingredients, such as crab or pig's tail, okra and hot peppers. The leaves are also simply cooked and served as a vegetable or mixed with rice, much in the same way as spinach.

Christophene Also known as chayote (and cho-cho in Jamaica), this pear-shaped squash has a delicate flavour and ranges in colour, though light green is the most common commercially available. The skin can be slightly prickly or smooth. The pip inside is edible but most people remove it and the skin before cooking. It can be eaten raw as well and is delicious in salads. The taste is similar to courgette, marrow and young squash.

Djon-djon A small black mushroom from North Haiti with a distinctive colour, flavour and aroma. Used to make the famous Haitian side dish 'riz djon-djon' (rice with mushroom), most often served with 'griots' (crispy pork chunks), fish or meat.

Palm hearts The edible inner part of the stem of the cabbage palm tree is called the heart. These mild-flavoured shoots are eaten both raw and cooked and are available canned from most delicatessens and West Indian shops as 'hearts of palm', 'chou palmis', or 'chou palmiste'. Palm heart has a similar texture to globe artichoke.

Plantain Like a large banana but without the sweetness, plantain must be cooked before it is eaten and is sold in varying stages of ripeness, from green to mottled and almost black. The mottled stage is the most flavoursome and sweetest. It is very versatile and can be boiled, baked or fried (see page 171).

Pumpkin The variety of pumpkin that is most often served in the Caribbean is the calabaza. It has a hard green and yellow skin and the colour of the flesh varies from yellow to bright orange.

STARCHES

Arrowroot A starchy powder obtained from the arrowroot plant, it is used as a thickening agent in soup, stews, sauce and glazes, and has no discernible flavour.

Cassava/manioc/yucca One of the traditional indigenous staple root vegetables of the Caribbean there are both bitter and sweet cassavas. It is made into a number of different products, including flour or meal, bread, 'cassereep' (see page 181) and tapioca, bitter cassava is used to produce 'bammies' – cakes generally eaten with fried fish. For exportation, cassava is coated in a wax-like substance which has to be peeled away with the skin. With sweet cassava, the root should then be split in half lengthways and the fibrous central stem should be removed before cooking.

Dasheen/taro This starchy tuber came originally from the South Pacific. It has a brown fibrous skin. The leaves are edible and referred to as callaloo (see page 230).

Eddoe/coco A small root vegetable with brown hairy skin and a grey or sometimes purplish flesh that, when cooked, has a distinctive nutty flavour, eddoe can be eaten hot, cold, in soups, roasted, mashed or pickled.

Sweet potato This edible tuber is grown throughout the tropics. The skin varies in colour from brown to deep pink to white and the flesh also varies from orange to greenish. It is extremely high in vitamins and can be found in many supermarkets today as well as specialist shops. It can be cooked in all the same ways as Irish or English potatoes. In America they are called sweet yams.

Yams Although the word yam is often used to cover many different tropical root crops it is in fact an edible tuber of plants of the genus Dioscorea. There are many different types of yam, varying in size, shape and colour. The flesh can also vary in colour from white, yellow, or pink or even purple. The bark-like skin may be smooth or rough, pale in colour or brown or purple. They have to be cooked before eating. Once cooked, they are fairly bland with a slightly sweetish flavour. They are used as a filling carbohydrate and can be steamed, boiled, mashed, grilled, roasted or fried.

Beans Throughout the islands, both fresh and dried beans or 'peas' are abundantly used. It would not be too much of an exaggeration to say that rice and beans are eaten at least once a day by most West Indians. They are a cheap and very healthy source of protein. Popular types include: red (kidney), black (kidney), pigeon peas, gungo peas (rather similar to pigeon peas; black-eyed beans can be used instead of either), broad beans and butter beans.

Cashew nuts Originally called acaju by the Amerindians, cashew shells contain poisonous liquid that must be drained off when harvesting the nuts. They can be eaten raw but are most often roasted and salted and eaten as snacks.

STAPLES

Cornmeal Cornmeal is used a great deal in Caribbean cooking for 'pastelles' or 'hallacas' (cormeal steamed in a banana leaf; the name varies from island to island, as does the filling), coocoo (cornmeal and okra pudding), bread, made into dumplings and desserts ('pone' and 'duckanoo') and cooked like polenta ('turned cornmeal').

Rice Rice is one of the most important staples in the Caribbean diet and it is eaten at least once day by most people. Rice is grown on a few of the islands where it is hot and wet: Dominican Republic, Cuba, Trinidad and Puerto Rico where it is generally used just for local consumption. Other islands have to import their rice.

SPICES AND FLAVOURS

Allspice/pimento Allspice or pimento is the dried berry of the pimento tree. The flavour is similar to a mixture of cloves, cinnamon and nutmeg. It is one of the core ingredients in jerk seasoning. It is used much in the same way as cloves, either whole (then removed before serving) or ground.

Annatto/roucou Sold in the form of a red powder or seeds, annatto/roucou is used as a colouring agent mostly with oil, which changes the colour of the food to a bright yellow-orange. It is often used as a cheaper substitute for saffron and has a mild, bland flavour. To make annatto oil, simply heat some annatto seeds in oil, allow to cool and then strain.

Chandon beni/culantro (Eryngium foetidium) A pungent wild herb used as a flavouring in many of the Spanish islands as well as in Trinidad, it is called by many different names: shadow bennie, shado beni, shadon bene and chandon beni. All seem to be descended from a French vernacular name, chardon beni, meaning 'blessed thistle', because it has thistle-like leaves. In Jamaica it is known as fit weed, as it is thought to cure 'fits'. Use coriander as a substitute.

Cinnamon/cassia (wild cinnamon) Cinnamon is the dried bark of a tree which is used as a flavouring for both sweet and savoury dishes. It is often combined with other herbs, for example, as one of the key ingredients in jerk seasoning. It is sold as strips of bark as well as a ground powder.

Clove This pungent spice, which is used in numerous dishes throughout the islands, both sweet and savoury, is cultivated in the Caribbean islands by the French and Dutch. The dry unopened buds resemble tacks or nails and the word 'clove' is derived from the Latin word for nail, *clavus*. It is available both whole and ground.

Cocoa/chocolate A successful crop in many islands for a number of years, until prices fell, which affected the commercial viability of the bean and many of the plantations closed. It is still grown in some islands, mostly for the domestic market. You will often see 'balls of cocoa' sold in small shops and in the markets. These are boiled in water or milk to make hot chocolate.

Coconut The coconut is the fruit of *Cocos nucifera* and it is used extensively in the Caribbean for both savoury and sweet dishes.

Coconut juice/water This is the liquid that is found in the centre of the fruit, which makes a cool and refreshing drink.

Coconut flesh (meat) When mature, coconut flesh is hard and cut be cut out and grated. It is covered with a thin membrane called the testa. When dried the mature coconut meat is called copra.

Coconut milk or cream A sweet liquid made by pouring hot water on to the grated coconut meat (see page 39). Other byproducts from the coconut used in cooking are coconut oil, coconut syrup and honey, made by reducing the milk with sugar.

Coriander/cilantro This pungent-tasting plant is part of the parsley family. It is often confused with flat-leaved parsley in appearance but the taste is quite different. The seeds are one of the ingredients in garam masala. Coriander is used extensively in the cooking of the Spanish islands. Use culantro as a substitute.

Curry/colombo Curry is found in many of the French and English islands of the Caribbean. It is especially popular in both Jamaica (curried goat) and Trinidad where it is most often sold in 'roti' flaps as a filling snack or light take-away meal. It is also very popular in Guadeloupe, where 'colombo de cabri' (goat curry) is a local speciality.

Fever grass/lemon grass Fever grass grows wild in the islands but until recently has only been used to make tea. However it is now beginning to be used as a flavouring in both sweet and savoury dishes.

Ginger This strong, peppery flavoured spice grows abundantly throughout the Caribbean and is used for flavouring both savoury and sweet dishes. Nowadays Jamaican ginger is believed to be one of the best in the world. It is also used to make tea as a cure for stomach ailments and also as a wine and 'ginger beer'. It is available both fresh (in the form of a knobbly root) and dry, as a ground powder, which is not as pungent.

Jelly This is the soft, jelly-like immature flesh inside the green coconut, which is scooped out and eaten as a snack after the coconut water has been drunk.

Molasses Molasses is a thick black sticky liquid which is a byproduct of the sugar cane industry. It is used to make rum, in desserts, cakes, pastries and sweets.

Mauby A refreshing drink with a bittersweet taste made from the infused bark of a tropical tree.

Nutmeg/mace Grenada is one of the world's main producers of nutmeg and mace. Nutmeg and mace come from the same nut of the nutmeg tree. When the fruit ripens the outer pericarp splits open to reveal the scarlet mace covering the brown nutmeg. When fresh, the mace is still pliable to strip off and dry. Mace is either sold dried or in powder form. The nutmeg must be shelled before it can be grated or ground into powder or crushed for the oil. Nutmeg and mace are used to flavour both sweet and savoury dishes as well as in many drinks.

Peppers It is the hot seasoning peppers that give Caribbean cooking its distinctive flavour. There are many different varieties and names, including bird pepper, country pepper and seasoning pepper but it is the scotch bonnet pepper, with its distinctive aroma and flavour, which is the most favoured in Jamaica. It is named after its resemblance to a little bonnet. Care should be taken when handling all hot peppers: do not touch your face or eyes after working with them and be sure to wash your hands thoroughly. If you are unable to find hot peppers, chilli peppers may be used but for a more authentic flavour, use hot pepper sauce.

Spring onion/escallion Spring onions are an integral part of any fresh seasoning in the islands.

Star anise A spice that reflects the Chinese influence in Caribbean cooking, star anise is a star-shaped dried fruit of *Illicium verum*. It is one of the ingredients in five-spice powder and is most often used in pork and chicken dishes.

Sugar cane This is a giant member of the grass family. The sugar is extracted by crushing the stems. Apart from sugar other byproducts include molasses from which rum is made. The juicy stem is deliciously sweet and refreshing and is often sucked or chewed to extract the juice.

Thyme Thyme is one of the most prolific herbs in the Caribbean. It is one of the main herbs used for seasoning of savoury dishes.

Vanilla Vanilla is used in many islands as flavouring for drinks and desserts. Most Caribbean vanilla comes from Puerto Rico.

SPECIAL FLAVOURS AND SEASONINGS

Adobo A Puerto Rican dry-rub seasoning combining garlic, oregano, salt and pepper, adobo is usually used on meat, especially pork. To make your own adobo seasoning, blend together 1 tsp onion powder, 1 tsp garlic powder, 1 tsp dried oregano and a pinch of salt and a pinch of pepper. Or make into a paste using vinegar and fresh ingredients.

Angostura Angostura bitters is a famous flavouring from Trinidad, whose ingredients are a closely guarded secret, though it is thought that tamarind pulp is one of them. Use a dash or two in sweets or savouries.

Ajili-Mojili A pungent sauce made from garlic, black pepper, hot pepper, lime and vinegar which is traditionally served with roast pork in Puerto Rico (see page 146).

Escoveitch A name for recipes derived from a traditional Spanish cooking technique for fish which is made by pouring a marinade of vinegar, onions, bay or allspice leaves and spices over grilled or fried fish. Escoveitch can be eaten either hot or cold.

Jerk seasoning The development of Jamaican jerk is credited to the Maroons, slaves who were abandoned by the Spanish during the British capture. Jerk was a method of seasoning and preserving their meat before smoking it over pimento leaves. Nowadays jerk seasoning is readily available in the shops and supermarkets in many different forms: dried, liquid marinade and traditional paste (see pages 118–147).

Sauce chien A simple sauce made from onion, garlic, chives, hot pepper, salt, black pepper and lime. In Guadeloupe it is used both as a seasoning before cooking and after cooking.

Ti-malice A popular Haitian hot pepper sauce.

SEAFOOD

Codfish/salt fish/morue pwason sale/poisson sale/bacalao The term codfish is generally applied to salted cod, which is imported into the Caribbean although it is part of the islanders' staple diet. The fish is soaked in water to remove the salt and then either boiled or roasted on a coal fire and seasoned with spices. It is used in many dishes throughout the Caribbean most famously for Ackee and Salt Fish in Jamaica (page 88), Bul Jol in Trinidad (page 47), akkra/ackra in Barbados, Haiti and Guadeloupe (see page 39 for preparation instructions). Canned salt fish is also available, usually called 'bacalao', which needs no preparation instructions.

Conch/lambie/lambi The most popular variety in the Caribbean is the queen conch, with its distinctively shaped shell, which is rosy pink inside. Conch meat can be eaten raw, marinated in lime, stewed and curried. Conch is most popularly associated with the Bahamas.

Crab Throughout the Caribbean there are many different species of crab but it is the 'land-crabs' that are considered the best. They are found where there is fresh water, in ponds and streams, and thrive in the many mangrove swamps. These are small crabs about 5–7.5 cm (2–3 inches) in diameter on average. The meat is often seasoned with spices and mixed with breadcrumbs and then stuffed back into the shells – 'crab backs'. They are also used to make callaloo soup, curries and stews.

Crayfish Several varieties of river crayfish, also known as freshwater shrimp and 'janga', can be found in the rivers of the Caribbean. The largest variety can be over 17 cm (7 inches) long.

Kingfish/wahoo/king mackerel A delicious meaty fish which is found in deep waters. It can be stewed, fried, baked and grilled.

Mackerel Canned and smoked mackerel are one of the staples in most Caribbean store cupboards. It was imported as a cheap source of food during the plantation era and remains popular today.

Marlin A popular game fish found in the water around Jamaica. Sometimes used as a substitute for salmon, as in smoked marlin.

Oysters Both sea oysters and mangrove oysters can be found in the Caribbean, though it is the oysters that attatch to trees in the mangroves that are the most popular with the islanders. They are generally sold by street vendors who open them on demand and serve them with a spicy tomato sauce with lime and hot pepper.

Red snapper Regarded as one of the finest fishes in the Caribbean, the medium-sized red snapper is very versatile; its firm, sweet flesh can be cooked in numerous ways, baked, grilled, fried, stewed and roasted.

Shark Fried shark served with 'bake' (fried bread) is an experience not to be missed if you visit Maracas Beach in Trinidad. This firm-fleshed fish can be curried, braised, fried and eaten raw in a ceviche with lime juice.

Tilapia Similar in taste to red snapper, this hybrid pink-skinned fish has become a very successful species for farming in Jamaica. It has a flavourful white flesh, which is considered quite a delicacy for many fish enthusiasts.

MEAT

Oxtail This cut of beef is hugely popular in the English-speaking islands, whose people pride themselves on their traditional family stews. In Jamaica, oxtail is often cooked with butter beans.

Salted beef/pork Salted meat was given to slaves on the plantation as part of their rations. It is still an important ingredient in traditional cooking and provide a unique flavouring for the many heritage recipes.

For additional advice on sourcing Caribbean food and ingredients, please refer to the Walkerswood web site, www.walkerswood.com.

glossary pictures

1. Ackees
2. Pomegranate
3. Red peas
4. Liquid roucou/annatto
5. Walkerswood pepper sauce
6. Land crabs
7. Ginger
8. Curry powder
9. Sweet potato
10. Habaneras
11. Cassava
12. Okras
13. Noni
14. Cinnamon bark
15. Guineps

Thank-yous *No project like this is possible without a great deal of support and input behind the kitchen curtains. Though there werre other helping hands along the way I must be especially thankful for the following:*

Evy Burke, my Mum, for the creativity, and Billy Burke, my Dad, who fed the curiosity. Roddy Edwards, Judy Bastyra, and Sandra Duhaney, who stood beside me. All the 'Jaguars' who love to cook and those who love to eat, my Sister Nancy Burke, Cindy Breakspeare, Andrea Hutchinson, Susan Parkinson, Alex Kerr-Wilson, Caryle Duffy, Myriam Portocarero, Maxine Walters, Annabella Proudlock, Vanessa Taylor, Suzanne Jobson, Suzette Robinson, JoyBell Dummett, Tobi Philips, Barbara Serlin, Pat Tracey and Michele Haynes – all those tasty parties! Woody Mitchell, Denyse Perkins, Johnny McFarlane, Ann Edwards, Myra Waugh, Celia Dixon Chambers, her daughter Kristina and the rest of the Walkerswood team, who gave their support. Cookie Kinkead, for lending her eye. Enid Donaldson, Norma Shirley, Johanna Thwaites, Sue Couch, Julius Chin Yee and Rosemary Parkinson – the culinary beacons along the way.

Special thanks to those who made some of the recent research so enjoyable:
Norma Llop and Isaac Zapata from the Puerto Rico Tourist Board, Blanche Gelabert, and Emilio Rivera and Chefs Joel Rodriguez and Roberto Trevino, grateful for your time. 5 stars to Marie France Leguier, who shared true Guadeloupian hospitality, Rony Theophile, for information, Simone Schwartz Bart, who opened her kitchen to us, Gigi Bourorga, Marie Celine and the funny Phillipe. Most grateful to Jag Mehta and Breezes staff in Curaçao; Dylene Esprit and Charla Nieveld from the Curaçao Tourist Board; Chef Michael Eusea, Maria and Janchi Christiaan. Without Brien and Grania deGannes, Trinidad would never be the same. Many thanks to Susie Montana, Gerrard Kenney, Kevin Kenney, Gilbert Bastyra, Steven Steele, Chefs Eli deSouza and Norris Marshall, and Piero Guerrini, who made it all so delicious.